HOW THE ALGARVE HAS CHANGED

A reflective look at this part of Portugal over the
past twenty seven years.

BRIAN J EVANS

authorHOUSE®

AuthorHouse™
1663 Liberty Drive
Bloomington, IN 47403
www.authorhouse.com
Phone: 1-800-839-8640

First published by AuthorHouse   08/24/2011

ISBN: 978-1-4567-8812-4 (sc)
ISBN: 978-1-4567-8813-1 (ebk)

Printed in the United States of America

CONTENTS

This book is dedicated to our one eared black and white cat called Fred.

ACKNOWLEDGEMENTS

I would to like to thank my wife Fay for her steadfast and continuous support in writing this book. Her razor sharp intelligent brain and incredible lateral thinking has been an inspiration and enormous support to me. I would like to think I could also say the same about my fourteen kids, that they would inspire me in the same way. But they have given me as much inspiration as a dead ferret! Saying you silly old fart you should be in a geriatric home, dribbling in a chair, not writing books! To the lady in the local shop (can't remember her name) who ripped me off with her prices while plying me with litres of diet Coke to quench my thirst whilst writing in the Portuguese (38%) heat. To my great aunt Mildred in Australia who thought she was inspiring me but I only crept around the 103 year old trout cos' she said she would leave me millions when she fell off the twig. Research later found she is poor as a church mouse with a gambling habit. The old biddy still refuses to croak. To my mum and dad, whoever they were, who left me to die in a wicker basket, (see 'about the author') as without their help I would never been born. To all the great authors in the world, whose brilliant works and exaggerated claims to fame and literary genius I have copied. Thanks to all the potential buyers of my book where the sales and royalties I might receive, could keep me in a lifestyle to which I would like to become accustomed: but probably not! To all my friends and acquaintances, who rolled about the floor exploding with laughter and fits of giggles when they heard I was trying to write a book! I am most grateful to Fred our one eared black and white cat, who insists on sitting on the keyboard of the computer when I am working and regularly presses the delete key and wipes off my last four hour's work!

And lastly to anyone reading this, we suggest that you now read 'About the author' then move on to the introduction, in order to bring a modicum of sanity back into your lives!

ABOUT THE AUTHOR.

B rian was born in 1941 to unknown parents when he was found in a wicker basket outside the Salvation Army offices just south of the entrance to Wigan Pier. After a year he was moved to the Convent of Our Lady Saint Oddballs in Goole. When he was five years old he was stolen from the Convent by Gypsies and was next seen performing in Billy Smart Circus as the Strong Man and Co-Co the Circus Clown.

After escaping from the circus he was educated at the University of Hard Knocks and obtained a First Class Master's Degree in Nothing at All (with Honours) His education continued when he became a highly paid mercenary Major General in the Welsh Civil War of Independence in 1971, gaining no distinction at all but was cashiered after having a bit of naughty with a buxom cook behind the bike sheds at the local Private Secondary School for Genteel Ladies.

He then held a number of highly respected positions as a professional Bungee Jumper, Beach Bum, general dilettante and nere-do-well travelling around the flesh spots of Europe, finally being elected as a Euro MP waiting for Tibet's inclusion in the European Economic Community.

He has never been married but has fathered fourteen children that he knows about, has thirty-one grandchildren and lost count of great grandchildren after the seventy third was born.

He now spends his time travelling between the UK and Portugal and is drunk as a skunk most of the time.

If these passages have brought a smile to your face then we will be delighted.

Seen here with Lorna his favourite granddaughter

Most of the photographs in the book are original and have been taken by Fay.

INTRODUCTION

Having owned a property in the Algarve for over twenty five years, been privileged to enjoy the delights of Portugal, its people and the Algarve in particular; we thought it would be useful for others contemplating such a move to read about my wife's and my special experiences in having a holiday home, with all the joys irritations and pitfalls that this venture brought to us. It is not supposed to be a tome of accurate detail and or fact, rather an emotional and somewhat biased view of Portugal dragged up from memory, as we travelled though our twenty seven year journey. In addition, a lot of the input may be based on local rumour, opinion and folk lore, which of course is far more interesting and juicy than fact, as the rumour machine is still alive and well in the Algarve! Also we hope to bring some humour (sometimes a bit warped or zany) and a sideways swipe at some of the stupidity and needless beaurocracy which we have encountered.

What most tourists, new residents and new comers generally fail to understand when travelling within the EU, and Portugal in particular, is that there are over two dozen languages, vastly different cultures, political structures and religious beliefs and there is no way, we can be fully involved as strangers and understand them, even if one also lives part of the time in their countries. Having been around the Algarve for many years, we still do not really fully comprehend our Algarve hosts cultures, traditions and values, which are of course very different from the rest of Portugal; especially as the Algarve was so influenced by Moorish domination many centuries ago.

Hopefully the reader will find that we have given an honest (perhaps sometimes too honest and outspoken) and unbiased view of the Algarve based on our experience, without the rose coloured spectacles from which many tourist/guide type books sometimes suffer. In addition it is difficult to write a book about a nation emerging from a dictatorship without mentioning some of the more negative aspects of the country and its administration, so bear with us in those sections; it is not all bad news! As Oliver Cromwell said 'Paint it again, warts and all'!

Other people may have different and sometimes better or worse experiences than us, but, for what it is worth, this is our story.

CHAPTER ONE

How it started

The British Airways aircraft stood on its stand with its auxiliary engine running and its entry door attached to the mobile air bridge. The silver fuselage and blue, red and white tailfin gleamed in the English drizzle at Gatwick Airport. This was in the days when British Airways, with its marketing catch phrase 'We take more care of you' was at its peak of popularity and really was the 'World's most favourite airline'. What twenty five years of cut throat competition, trades union entrenched practices and poor management can do to such a successful airline! It is all very sad. We looked out of the lounge window on this really miserable, dank October day in 1984 and thought how wonderful it will be to leave the UK for a one week holiday in the sun.

I had been working at full stretch for the past nine months, to the point of a complete nervous and physical breakdown. My management consultancy business was doing very well since starting it in 1977 and the client base had grown to the point where I should be employing addition advisors to help with the ever burgeoning workload. But of course, like many small businessmen felt that I could manage OK. My company, Industrial Relations and Personnel Services Ltd, was a roaring success since its inception. However, success had come at a price and that price was my health. Totally knackered!

'Fay please find somewhere in the sun where we can crash out and recharge our batteries' I had asked my wife and PA some weeks before. So, in her normal efficient way she had booked the break. In those days it was no mean feat to arrange a holiday. It was a ten minute car journey to the local travel agent, sit for hours choosing from dozens of holiday brochures, the agent would then have to phone or fax the holiday company. We would then go home for the night. After many telephone calls, other visits to the agent, the writing of cheques and the delay until the cheque cleared, the deal was done. These days we find the holiday on the internet, press a couple of buttons on the computer, pay for it by credit card and it is all done!

As we boarded the aircraft, I asked where we were going and Fay said 'Portugal'. Didn't mean a thing to me at the time, it could have been Timbuktu. As the plane taxied and took off, I fell asleep. Cannot remember much about the flight but as we came into land in the sun at Faro airport, where we had never landed before, Fay looked out onto the mud flats on the landing approach and said in a very anxious loud voice, 'We are going to land on the mud' which are the mud flats on the approach to the airport. She had always been nervous of flying and this was one of the few flights she had made since steeling herself to agree to international travel by air. After this trip air travel began to cost us a small fortune and sometimes my bank account wished I had never persuaded her to give it a try. As the plane taxied to a halt, we expected to walk off onto the normal air bridge as we would in the UK but not a bit of it. We were to learn over many years in the future, we would be bussed from the aircraft to the arrivals lounge in a cramped coach full of passengers, standing up, strap-hanging like the London underground railways!

This was a new experience for us both. To call the arrivals lounge a lounge in those days, was an overstatement. The airport was little more than a collection of badly built huts! We found this very strange but in our ignorance did not realise that the overthrow of the Salazar dictatorship regime and the removal of the Communist government, was only nine years earlier and not only was the airport like a third world shanty, so was the rest of the country. However, by the time we had cleared customs and met our holiday rep, it was beginning to get dark. We were shepherded through to the exit, to what looked like a very cramped car park full of taxis. The situation was chaotic! There were people pushing and shoving, very little organisation and the rep trying to find the driver who would take us to our rented Villa. This took forever!

Eventually we were ushered into a car, which we assumed was a taxi. As it started to leave the airport in the dark, with the driver not speaking any English (no reason that he should, after all he was Portuguese) we started to wonder if this foreign holiday was a good idea. Should we have gone to Butlins at Skegness? The journey to the Villa which we had booked in Quinta Das Raposeiras Santa Barbara, some fifteen miles from the airport, was driven at breakneck speed until the last ten minutes, when the driver was trying to find the address. We drove in the gloom higher and higher up what we thought was a mountain and wondering if this feller really know where he was going. After a lot of muttering and cursing, turning around many times after losing his way, we arrived at Casa Salamanca around 8.30 pm tired, nervous and apprehensive. Threw all our bags in the bedroom, had a very large glass of wine which the owners had left for us, got into bed and went straight to sleep, pooped!

The next morning was a revelation. Falling out of bed around 9.00 am, we surveyed the white washed detached Villa which we thought was magnificent. Marble floors all over, three on-suite bathrooms, large terrace and a swimming pool and what seemed to us a tropical garden. We thought we had arrived in heaven. After a leisurely breakfast with food the Villa owners had left for us (these days holiday makers would find it very unusual to have a welcome pack of food and wine) we repaired to the pool terrace, semi naked. The sun was beating down, with a temperature of 30 degrees, without a cloud in the sky. The views over the wooded and farmed hills to Faro were magnificent, the peace and quiet was unbelievable, just the place to crash out and recharge the batteries. Out came the suntan cream, towels and sunglasses and we were like pigs in a trough! We tried the water in the pool and it was freezing! Fay asked why I thought it was too cold in which to swim. With all my vast knowledge of the Algarve and swimming pools, never having been there before, I said that it had probably only just been filled!!! What an ignorant Pratt. Little did we know that soon after September, the water cools to a very low temperature and it was, very cold.

Anyway, nothing mattered in this Nirvana and we sunbathed, listening to the Beatles 'She Loves You' song played by the James Last orchestra on a Walkman tape player (CDs had not been invented) Lunchtime arrived and I said to Fay 'Would you like to have a Villa here? Yes OK was the reply! No real thought was put into the decision but the way we made decisions in our business was normally very fast, so the die was cast! The holiday rep came to see us late in the day to see if all was well and at the same time bringing our hire car, a Mini, a matter that we will return to later under vehicles. We expressed an interest in building a house and immediately he recommended, in his view, a good honest reliable builder called Fernando Martins who spoke very good English.

Early the next day, there was a knock on the door and the salesman from the building company, called Feliciano Martins arrived to talk about the process of building the house. He was the half-brother of Fernando and arranged for us to meet him to discuss the feasibility and to look at building plots. We then spent most of our holiday week travelling around the area with Fernando, looking at land that we could afford and what we thought would be a nice area.

We had heard horror stories about Brits being ripped off by builders, mostly in Spain, so we were very cautious in trusting anyone. So we made extensive enquiries wherever we could about the Fernando's reputation, checked his office location and all contacts we made said the he was honest, reliable and a good chap as the rep has stated. We eventually settled on a plot two thirds up an unmade dirt road on a hillside in a small hamlet called

Gorjoe's, (pronounced Gorsshoyns, some of the Portuguese language is very difficult to get the tongue around) near Santa Barbara and Loul'e. The plot was a delight, small, sloping, and faced west, surrounded by enormous dry stone walls some two metres high and two meters thick, so they ensured privacy from the other plots. It boasted beautiful country and panoramic sea views, with only four houses along the length of the unmade mud track. We called the house Casa Colina Sonolenta, which roughly translated meant, 'House On The Sleepy Hillside' Our plot was to be the last to be built up the hill and on asking Fernando if there could be any further houses built, he said that that would not be possible because there was only a small donkey track past us and that would not support lorries etc! Obviously this was one of the three great lies in life. One—here is a man from head office, he is here to help you! Two—Your job is safe and you will not be made redundant! Three—they will never build up there! Now twenty seven years later, there are a total of thirteen more houses built past us up the hill! Some of them real Gin Palaces complete with tennis courts and very intrusive floodlights!

We agreed the plans for the house, a modest detached dwelling, two bedrooms, a sitting room with an open fire in the corner, kitchen and one bathroom, a 10 x 5 metre swimming pool and terraces, all for the inclusive price with the land of £35,000.00. A similar dwelling today would cost around £250.000.00 if one could find one of similar size, as these days houses are built very much larger. The sale was agreed without a deposit, on a handshake with Fernando. Sometime later we asked if a garage could be built at the end of the pool. Not many houses had garages in those days, and Fernando again, shook hands on the additional build and he said he would construct it as a gift to us at no charge. Unbelievable! Later we paid the deposit, signed a promissory note and found that the lawyer appointed to deal with the legal aspects of the sale, was Fernando's wife Ilda. A lovely formidable lady, a very qualified lawyer, well respected in the Algarve and in some areas, feared for her contacts and successes in the law courts. We have continued to use her services all the time we have been in the Algarve.

All new properties in Portugal have to be built to withstand earthquakes since the terrible one which demolished two thirds of Lisbon in 1755. This means constructing a reinforced concrete and steel structure able to withstand earth tremors, which takes a considerable time to build. As the house was situated on a rocky hillside with many large boulders to be excavated, there were some delays waiting for a licence to use dynamite to blast some of the hill away. Some of the holes drilled into the stone are still visible today. Progress was slow and it took around ten months to build and as far as we could see, with our limited knowledge of Portuguese building methods, was finished to a very good standard.

The one issue we did not understand at the time was the way the sewers were installed. In the UK every step the builders make in laying drains and sewers is checked by the council building inspectors and nothing can be signed off until everything is correct and they give their approval. We found to our cost many years later that this is not the case in Portugal. The builders lay the sewers through to the cess pit without any thought as to how they will be cleared in the future. The pipes are of a smaller diameter than the UK, block much easier and where they put the inspection boxes, is still a mystery even to the Portuguese. In nearly every case the boxes are covered over by terrace tiles so nobody can tell where they are. In one case in another Villa, the drain clearing people found the box under the sitting room floor! So twenty years later when tree roots and other unmentionable objects have blocked the drains, we spend many happy hours with arms covered in rubber gloves up to the armpits, rummaging down the sewers and spending lots of Euros trying to clear the blockages!

One of the strange things about building houses in Portugal, is because of the need for reinforced concrete pillars, there is no damp proof course laid, so in low lying areas in the winter months, the damp can creep up the walls. We understand that with more modern construction this problem has been overcome. As our house was built on a rocky hillside, the water drains away from the house so we did not ever have this problem.

The mud track to our plot was very pretty, winding up the hill with natural Olive, Carob and Palm trees on each side of the road. Above our site on the next piece of land was a broken down ruin of a house with only the four outside walls standing. All around the top of the walls, plants and green vegetation hung down, with some of the rendering breaking away, making the remains look in a very sad state. When it was first built the original roof would have been pitched with wooden rafters covered in red tiles and must have been owned by a relatively wealthy Portuguese: as one of the signs of wealth in those days was to have an apex roof which of course was more expensive to build than the normal flat type. Another feature of wealth was the size and complexity of design of the chimney. The more fancy filigree work built into its design, the more it would cost to build. We understand that one could build the chimney and have it priced by the day, so a three day one would cost more than a one day effort, therefore the longer it took to build the more it cost; so the more obvious affluence the owner could display. The chimney of the ruin was very large and complex.

Our builder did not believe that it would ever be re built as the whole structure was very damp and tumbling down. Some years later a lovely German couple fell in love with the site and the house and spent a small fortune renovating it to its formal glory; it is now a very up market dwelling and is probably worth quite a sum.

How builders working practices and hours of work have changed over the years. When houses were being built in '84 the workmen would appear on site between 7.00am to 8.00am, in the cool of the morning and arrive on very noisy motorbikes, waking all and sundry. They would then work until around 1.00pm, have a two to three hour lunch, cook a very substantial meal over an open wood fire, have a sleep in the shade, then continue working until about 7.00pm then go home. Now they arrive quietly in their cars at 8.00am, have a one hour lunch break in the local bar and finish at 5.00pm. How sensible in this summer heat!

A measure of how things have changed over time is the advancement in the technology of workman's tools. As we watched the house being built, the only real mechanisation was the petrol or electrically driven cement mixer and a noisy JCB. Most small tools were hand operated and what a joy it was to see and hear the swish of a wood plane as the shavings curled onto the floor and the rasping of a hand saw as it cut through timber, with the lovely fragrance of freshly cut pine wood. Now nearly all tools are electrically powered and we now hear the whine of the electric plane and the screaming of the rotary rip saw. But then this is progress and the workmen are all the better off for the change.

We asked Fernando if the mains water which we expected to be laid to the house was safe to drink and to our horror he said that water would be delivered in a tanker and poured into an underground concrete systerna. The sewerage he explained would end up in a cess pit which will never be emptied! We were horrified at the thought. So from that day to this only bottled water has been drunk, at great expense! Wine at this time could be bought for some £1.00 per bottle and water not much cheaper. So, no contest there, the wine won very time!

It is still possible to buy wine at really rock bottom prices for around €1.50 a bottle and the quality is so much better than it was in '84.

So with the house being finished, we moved in during November 1985.

The next challenge was to equip our new holiday home with furniture and fittings, which we later found to be very sparse and utilitarian compared with England.

So our love story with the Algarve began.

CHAPTER TWO

House furnishing

We expected to quickly find a furnishing store to buy all the furniture and curtains etc. under one roof as we would in the UK, something like John Lewis.

Innocents abroad were we! Trying to find a comfortable divan bed was impossible. The traditional bed was four hardwood timber legs joined together with a wood frame with inflexible wood struts laying dovetailed across the frame, all held together with screws and bolts. On top of this, was an extremely hard mattress that invariably did not fit the size of the wooden frame. The good news was that we could buy the most elaborately hand carved, hardwood mahogany bed head for next to nothing. Our headboard bought when we moved in, these days would be very hard to find and would cost a small fortune. Nowadays it would be considered an antique. We still have the original in use and it is well polished and treasured.

Most other furniture was manufactured in traditional hardwood, usually utilitarian, highly polished and usually pretty uncomfortable, although very reasonably priced. Buying curtains was a complete mystery. Not the ready-made types we were used to at home. We met a lovely

couple, Robert and Susan of Lady Susan's Restaurant in
Faro, who we will refer to later under vehicles, who said
that one of the only places that we could buy curtains
was a shop called Bambinela's in Faro. So we pitched up
expecting to get them off the shelf. Oh no! A miserable
selection of dowdy materials, very old fashioned and
not to our taste but that was the choice. Not only that,
they had to do the whole job. They came to the house
to measure up and make the curtains, supply the wooden
poles (which we are still using) then some weeks later,
supply and install them! A job we would have normally
undertaken ourselves.

Kitchen equipment was very basic, consisting of an
electric cooker which in the UK we would have thrown
in the tip, plus a stainless steel sink unit. Hot water was
heated by an emersion heater in the kitchen. There was
no heating in the house, except for the open log fire and
as we only came to the house in the summer months,
we assumed that the country was always hot all the year
round. How wrong could we have been! Robert and Susan
counselled us to put heating into the house, but the only
times we had been in the Algarve was when it was hot so
we thought that it was mild all the year round. But we just
laughed at their suggestion. We then came in December
and realised that we were going to be really cold so went
into Faro to buy heaters. Whilst we were struggling to get
the heaters into the car we saw Robert and Susan and
they just smiled a wry smile. Were we embarrassed! See
the chapter on weather.

The choice of sitting room chairs was very limited,
mostly very basic, lacking in any style other than traditional

Portuguese and uncomfortable. Nearly all settees came fitted with a 'put u up' bed which, in fact was well constructed and worked very efficiently for when we had additional guests. Selecting furniture in the stores was a new experience. Most of the shops did not have the lights on during the daytime in order to save electricity, so we did not know whether they were open or shut. Once inside, the assistant would turn on the lights and then follow us around almost glued to our sides, in case we wanted to ask any questions. We found this most off putting, as it did not give us the opportunity to think clearly or discuss our views of the merchandise. So we decided that the best thing to do was to split up and both of us go in different directions. This seemed to confuse the assistant as they had to decide which one of us held the purse strings and then follow them! One of the first phrases in Portuguese we learned was 'We are just looking'. Once we left the store the lights were turned off. This practice still exists today but is confined mostly to owner run businesses. In larger, newer chain stores these days as in the UK, it is unusual to find an assistant to get any help.

It was so difficult to get the normal furnishings we expected which we could easily obtain in the UK, bed sheets were all very different sizes and in order to get what we wanted we had to bring them out from England. White plastic sun loungers were like gold dust and we bought them from the UK in the aircraft hold together with a microwave oven, as these were just not obtainable in Portugal.

Now there are large multi departmental furnishing stores as we would expect in the UK but are still few and far between. The best one is called Conforama near Gia. Still there are the one off owner occupied specialist furniture shops but prices tend to be sky high.

One of the latest developments in the Algarve are company's specialising in transporting English goods from the UK, to be delivered to one's own address in Portugal and will arrive within one week. A settee of reasonable quality priced in Portugal at around €1800.00 can now be bought in the UK for about €800.00 and when adding the transport price of about €150.00 the finished price is so much lower and we get the same or better quality. So many folks are now using this service. We know of some families who even order all of their groceries every week from the UK by this method!

Sadly, a lot of small furniture shops are closing down due to the difficulty of paying high rents; they suffer from less turnover of stock and fierce competition from the multinationals, hence lower profits.

However, we completed the furnishing of the house to a very high standard and it did look stunning in a very traditional Portuguese style.

There are now much more modern and contemporary furniture shops and shopping centres. The new Forum shopping and leisure centre in Faro is complete with a nine screen cinema with a 3D screen. When it initially opened, a single film would be shown and it would run from beginning to the end, as we would expect in the UK. Soon the Portuguese (who do not seem to be great film goers) complained that there was no interval where they could go out for a smoke and a drink. So now the film runs until about half way through, usually at the most exciting part, then stops without warning for the interval! The lovely part about the films in Portugal is that most are in English with the Portuguese language in subtitles, even with our limited knowledge of the language, the translation of the words, do leave something to be desired. In 1984 there was only a few cinemas, which were very small, had a restricted list of films and very uncomfortable. This new concept is wonderful.

In the winter months the paved pedestrian area, is converted into a winter wonderland with a gigantic white Christmas tree reaching to the top of the building and decoration all around the centre; plus a full size ice skating rink which is a great favourite with the Portuguese people. These facilities could only be dreamt of prior to the EU and the fall of the Salazar dictatorship.

The Quinta (pronounced Kinta) Shopping centre at Quinta Do Lago, is complete with restaurants, bars and very up market shops where we can buy furniture, with high prices to scare the pants off most holidaymakers.

Having furnished the house it was now time to experience the culinary delights of the area.

CHAPTER THREE

Alcohol and Restaurants

In all the bars and restaurants then, as now, one can buy an alcoholic drink at any time of the day or night when the establishment is open, and why not? Not so in the UK where opening times are restricted, where alcoholism is a real problem and drunken loutism both with guys and gals has become a feature of UK life. We have never experienced these problems with the Portuguese people, although we suspect that they may exist in some of the more downmarket resorts. Locals will go out in families to restaurants and bars with all ages mixing together without any apparent social problems. They drink in moderation and have a great time without getting drunk. This was so in 1984 and has not changed to this date.

We have only seen three instances of drunks in twenty seven years, two have been totally harmless and all very funny. The first was when we first came to Faro to watch the progress of the house being built. We stayed in the Eva Hotel opposite the Faro Marina and went to bed around 11.00pm. At around 3.00am, we were woken with a jolt to hear and see an elderly Portuguese man drunk as a Lord, staggering past the hotel, singing at the top of his voice, playing the spoons and falling all over the place. He was harmless, having a great time and not interfering with anybody. The second happened only two years ago in Santa Barbara De Nex'e, where there had been a social event and two young lads were the worse for wear with too much alcohol. In other words they were rolling drunk. They were holding each other up, laughing and giggling, falling into the road, then helping each other up before falling over again, grappling with each other all over the road, laughing all the time and not hurting or interfering with anyone. The third is covered in miscellaneous

The first restaurant we went to on our initial week holiday was called 'The Dock' on the Marina in Faro and it was one of the few in the area. The owner did not speak any English and the whole meal was ordered by sign language, with much waving of arms and pointing. The kitchen served the most magnificent shellfish and seafood in very Portuguese style. We went for the Sea Bream but of course, in those days the only accompaniment was boiled rice and potatoes with green vegetables. With our, by then, superb sign language, we asked for chips (French Fries for the posh) and not only was the waiter staggered that we wanted such food, he explained with much gesticulating of hands and body language that chips were almost unheard of in the Algarve and only boiled potatoes were served. Now it is very difficult to get any food that does not have chips served as standard, boiled potatoes have to be ordered as a special.

Now there are so many restaurants in the area that we could eat out at a different one every night of the year and not go to the same one twice. Although with the current recession, a lot of them are disappearing like snowballs in the summer. When the European Cup was staged in Portugal the restaurateurs thought they were on to a gravy train and would make a fortune during the playing of the matches. The prices went through the roof and where meals were priced around €10.00 before the matches, they doubled to over twenty, that was without wine and in very downmarket establishments. The more expensive were even more extortionate. Well, the obvious happened; the public decided that those prices were not for them and stayed away in droves leaving the restaurants virtually empty. Now with the recession, prices have dropped like a stone and a meal can be priced at around €7.50 and falling and they are still struggling to make a living.

There is a bar/restaurant in Santa Barbara called The Aportada (the gateway) and is the watering hole for a large percentage of locals and holidaymakers alike. It is a stunning location set in the centre of the village which as the name suggests, is entered by a large archway with wrought iron gates, leading to an extremely attractive outside eating area, covered in green vine type plants with multi scented flowers hanging over the dining tables. Inside it is decorated in traditional Portuguese style with dining for the winter months with a stage where occasionally the local dramatic society will put on very acceptable and professional shows. Within the waiting area is the bar which is well stocked and in front of it, has half a dozen very high wicker bar stools.

Many years ago there were a number of locals who used to meet there and were called 'The Sunday Club'; they were a group of English people in their latter years and all went to the church not a hundred metres away in the village. They used to go to the bar after the communion service, for their Sunday midday drink. They were not big drinkers and would sit for hours nattering over a half litre of beer, much to the annoyance of mine host. The exception was a rather rotund lady of very mature years who would regularly have far too much to drink, slur her words and eventually fall of her bar stool with a hell of a thump on the floor. The remainder of the Sunday Club would then stagger around trying to re seat her on the stool. This became something of a tourist attraction, with the other regulars who would watch and take bets on how long it would take before she fell off!

This went on for some years until the owner got fed up with the meagre amounts of money they were spending and much to the Club's chagrin, were all banned from the bar for ever. The owner at the time was an elderly gentleman who had the reputation of being a bit of an old soak himself and rumour had it, that if you went in there you could get well sloshed by breathing in his alcoholic breath. He eventually sold the bar to a sheep farmer from the north of England who ran it for many years. He did not know much about running a restaurant but a lot about sheep. It is now run by an Italian chap who majors on Italian food and it is very popular.

Some years ago a really weird and hilarious situation happened in a very well-known restaurant in Almancil, which has the pretention to be a bit Italian but is not. Obviously we cannot name the place as we would probably get sued for defamation of character. We arrived around seven thirty pm to find the restaurant empty, which is nothing unusual at that time of night. Having seated ourselves at the table of our choice, the waiter arrived with menu and wine list. He was a short little man with an enormous handlebar moustache, quite elderly and a bit smelly, with a smattering of English. He left us to consider our choice and returned some time later to take our order. We chose the main course and when it came to order the wine, as we always do, chose the house wine as it is always good value and reasonably priced (cheap). He then went into his sales spiel about some of the more expensive options and how wonderful they were. No thank you we said, we will stick with our first choice. At that point his body language said it was obvious that he was not a happy bunny, so he let out an enormous fart (flatulence for the posh). We thought poor old soul he has probably had too much brown bread! He then continued to try and push the more expensive wines, to which we very politely and firmly said no thank you. Then he farted again. Well, by this point we were in fits of uncontrollable giggles. So, off he went with his tail between his legs to place our order.

We were still in fits of laughter when a family of four arrived and as usually happens; they chose a table right next to ours, although there were empty tables all over the place. Anyway, smelly waiter turns up to take their order and they too ordered the house wine, to which he farted again! He tried the same sales pitch about the more expensive wine, they too refused and at this point he let out another enormous fart. By this time we were shaking uncontrollably and the other diners also were in fits of giggles. How he could fart to order we could not understand. Needless to say we never dined there again!

Dotted along the beaches from Faro to Villamoura and set directly on the sandy dunes were numerous beach bars, all majoring in sea food but with some very acceptable meat and chicken dishes. Most of them were little more than wooden and corrugated iron shacks with loads of character, not very clean but with very reasonably priced food. One comes to mind which did not have a name but the regulars called it 'The Brazilian' due to the high number of them working as waiting staff. The food was mediocre, the service slow but the atmosphere was noisy and electric. After all the meals were served, the diners well-oiled and the tables cleared, the waiters would appear with various musical instruments, drums, guitars, accordions etc. and they would really have a ball with all the diners dancing and singing along with the staff into the early hours.

Another was a smidgen up market but not much, again served excellent seafood and tourists had heard its reputation from friends who had returned to the UK, had raved about the quality of the food and its reasonable prices. It was always packed from lunchtime to late. The views of the sandy beaches and the seascapes were magnificent, especially with the sun setting over the ocean. People could come directly off the beach, have a meal and return to the beach between courses.

Unfortunately for the restaurant owners and diners, these beaches were part of the nationally protected Rio Formosa natural wild-life park, which is home to many unusual and rare migrating birds and wild animals. The authorities in their wisdom decided that the view along the beaches should not be obstructed by these 'unsightly and unhygienic' beach bars and restaurants, so at a stroke they had to be pulled down and moved back from the beaches at least fifty metres, then rebuilt with concrete bases and more modern wooden structures with hygienic toilets etc. which had all the atmosphere of a dead dog! So we lost some of the best tourist attractions, many of the new buildings do not have a good view, if any, of the beach and ocean.

Vale do Lobo beach from the Sandbanks restaurant/bar which is one which we enjoy most.

However, some bars which were on the beach but not obstructing the views as decreed by those who know best, have survived and, as they have a monopoly of the beach bars, can name their price for their services. At one such bar, which must remain nameless for obvious reasons, the owner has decided that he wants to retire a multi-millionaire if his charges are to be believed. Most menu's in the Algarve give a food price which is complete, so Sea Bream for example will come with potatoes, boiled or chips, vegetables or salad of your choice. Not this cheeky chappie, he gives the price on the menu, say Sea Bream €18.00, not bad you think but at the back of the menu there is the price of the 'extras', which most people do not see; chips €3.50. Veg €3.50 salad €3.50 etc. Then when one orders Sea Bream, he aske's, 'would you like potatoes?' yes please 'veg'? yes please, so instead of €18.00 the final bill could be €28.50!! Multiply this by a table of six diners, €171.00!! Wow what a shock for a family on a reduced budget!

We watched one gentleman who was obviously mine host to his large family of children and grandchildren, telling them to have anything they liked on the menu, which they did. When the bill came he looked horrified and his tan turned white with the price. He passed the slip to his wife who promptly pulled out a calculator to add up the price, which of course was correct so he had to pay up and look big. Bet he never goes to that bar again! Thankfully there are very few of these types of owners in the Algarve.

Another bar which remained on the beach quite a way from Ria Formosa was call the Black Horse Bar/Restaurant on the Loul'e beach which of course is miles away from Loul'e. It served excellent seafood, Piri Piri chicken and chips, was right on the beach and diners could watch their children playing on the sand in complete safety. It was very popular with locals and holidaymakers and was always packed at lunchtime, so to get a seat we had to get there early. The Bar was rather a ramshackle affair with loads of atmosphere, built of timber, with a corrugated tin roof and had adequate shaded areas to protect some tables from the sun whilst leaving others in the full glare. Sadly one winter, there were so many storms that the sea eroded the foundations of the building and it collapsed and had to be pulled down. So another beach bar bit the dust!

Another restaurant owner who wanted to get rich quick ran a very expensive Chinese restaurant not far from the beach. It was always packed and we had several meals there which were not memorable but OK. This particular evening we were served by five different waiters, the service was slow and the food not too hot. When the bill came it was around €60.00, but added on the bottom in hand written biro was an additional €11.50. So we challenged the cashier and asked what this was for. Service she said. So we said we had not had any service and complained that the service was as stated above. After some very cross words from both of us she took the extra money off the bill! We don't mind paying good money for good food and service but we object to being ripped off! Needless to say this establishment closed soon after. There is a surprise!

Having now tasted the food in the local restaurants we now had to start buying our own food from the supermarkets.

CHAPTER FOUR

Food and markets

I n 1984, in and around all the small villages and hamlets there were dotted Minimercado's, mini food stores. They were situated close enough for the locals to walk to and carry their shopping bags back to their houses. There were no supermarkets as we understand them, like Tesco's, Waitrose's and Sainsbury's. They just did not exist in the Algarve. We were so unused to the sparse array of very poor quality food and provisions that we were shocked to find so many goods that we could not buy. Quite often the fruit and veg they sold was brought in and sold to the store by locals who had grown them in their gardens. Sometimes the produce which was not sold would be left on the shelves to the point that they would be inedible. No perfectly shaped oranges and apples etc. without a blemish that we were used to, although those on sale were very tasty and sometime quite misshapen and ugly. Tea bags were awful and still are not to our taste and to this day we still bring them from England. On the first holiday, we went without sugar for three weeks because we could not find the familiar packet of Tate and Lyle on the shelves, then we realised it was sold in a brown paper cartons. So every time we went out to a bar for coffee, we would take home the spare packets of sugar supplied with the drinks.

Sometimes in '84 it was very difficult for a stranger to identify a shop, as there was quite often no shop name shown, so it was not always easy to know what was being sold. Normally the only entrance was through a very narrow door and there was no window to display the goods or show what produce they were selling; they were also very hot in the summer and extremely cold in the winter. We guess that they were built that way to save money when building and to keep out the heat in the summer. In the smaller villages even today they have not changed, although the more progressive and modern thinking business people have started to install plate glass windows and air conditioning.

As in the UK, with increasing affluence of the populace they began to buy motor cars and could shop further afield from their villages, so larger supermarkets began to appear; very slowly at first, with the opening of one in Faro called Modelo around 1990. We could not believe our luck, so every time on the first morning after our arrival in Portugal, it was in the car and into Faro, twenty kilometres away and buy our provisions for the whole stay. Inevitably, these larger supermarkets with their enormous buying power, cut the prices of the goods sold in the mini-markets, offered more choice and better quality, so the local markets began to suffer and close. This has been such a shame as they were an integral part of village life and great centre for communication and village gossip. One such min-market was Marias Deli in Gorjoe's. There were five local food shops plus a butcher's in the area, all owned and run by local people. Maria and her husband Raol were Portuguese born and lived in America for many years and had returned to the area where they were born, due to an accident that Raol had suffered whilst working in the US. She opened a small butchers shop quite close to where we stayed and was a very adept butcher. However, having experienced the lifestyle in the USA she was much more aware than most, of what customers wanted from a store, especially as at this time there was a significant number of English and other Europeans buying holiday homes in the area.

At first, in addition to selling her meat, she started to display eggs which the locals bought in for her to sell. Then some mushrooms appeared on the counter, then some oranges. More food was then stocked until eventually she enlarged the shop and turned it into a small mini market very similar to others in the area. But there was a significant difference. Europeans started asking for the food they would have bought in their own country and although Maria did not have a clue as to what they were asking for, she would research the products and find a supplier, then supplied their needs, obviously at a price! So after many years of listening to her clients the business grew and grew to a point where she expanded the building to the size of a small Waitrose with an enormous choice of international foods. The other small Mini Markets still held their traditional stock for the locals and with Marias Deli and the large supermarkets competition, they were really struggling. The inevitable happened; the smaller shops began to close with the loss of the 'heart' of the villages. Maria reached retirement age and sold the Deli, we assume at a very good price, to a supermarket chain called Ali Super. They ran it very badly for the next five years then closed it. Last year this chain went bankrupt and all the stores have closed. The building still remains for sale in a very dilapidated state and with the demise of the other shops the soul of the area is sadly disappearing.

One of the more successful supermarkets to open in the area, was, and is still is run by Portuguese, catered for the wealthy holidaymakers, the golfing fraternity and it was the only supermarket of any note. Its prices have always been very high and always packed with people. It is so highly priced, locals call it 'Costalot' but it did stock a lot of English food that was not on sale anywhere else. Now there is huge competition from another major store which opened recently and 'Costalot', out of the holiday season is almost empty of shoppers. Well, they had the good days and now with the current recession, we guess they are they are feeling the draft. As an example of the wide range of prices: Cucumbers in Costalot are priced at €5.99, in Pingo Doce €1.29 and in England 85P and they are all imported from Spain!

Many of the local open air and covered markets situated in small towns and village centres in earlier days, were stocked by locals bringing in home grown produce (and still are) but the ambience left a lot to be desired. Health, safety, hygiene, and air conditioning were not quite at the top of the list, leaving them quite hot and smelly but they did have loads of character. In recent years most have been vastly upgraded and modernised which took years to do and whilst they have lost a lot of their character and charm, are much more user friendly, safe and hygienic. When the Loul'e market was being renovated they closed the only undercover car park in the town and moved the whole market into the car park. What a sensible idea!

Stocks of food and the range of goods have improved and prices have remained reasonably steady in spite of competition from the larger supermarket chains. However, the cost of refurbishment must have been astronomical (we assume grants from the EU have helped) running into millions of Euros; but in our view are all the better for the change.

The outdoor Gypsy markets continue to survive in most towns although the largest was in Loul'e, was situated behind the main street, covered a huge amount of 'car parking' ground and was a great draw for tourists who came from miles around in coaches. Saturdays, which are the only days when the markets are open, are packed with holiday makers and locals alike. The GNR always have had a high presence looking for stolen and counterfeit goods and do have some success. They still have the Gypsies manning the stalls and they continue to give the spiel, 'I give you very good price missy' routine, yeah, if you believe that you'll believe anything! The regular cry of 'everything five euros' entices us to buy. Although one enterprising guy has his sales talk recorded on a tape machine and is very repetitive if we stand in the same area too long. We can buy anything from a complete set of hand or garden tools to a pair of knickers. As the need for building space has increased in the town and flats built on the open spaces, the markets have increasingly been moved further out of town and have become smaller, so there is not so much interest from people.

We have experienced many of these Gypsy markets in different parts of Europe and it seems that all of the products they have on offer look exactly the same and similar prices. We suspect that somewhere in the world there are factory sweat shops churning out the goods manned either by illegal immigrants or child labour working for peanuts!

One of the fascinating aspects of the markets, are the street musicians who play in and around the markets. One such group is called Wiracoocjha and they play rather lovely haunting South American Andes music, on many varied Pan Pipes, flutes tambourines and similar instruments. We saw them playing in Loul'e one August and when we travelled to Italy to ski the following February, to our complete surprise, they were playing in the Cervinia Ski resort, which lies in the lee of the Matterhorn, with snow falling all around, albeit they were wearing much warmer clothes than they did in the Algarve!

One of the strange market issues at present is that of the sale of oranges. For years Portugal has sold its oranges to Spain and it has always been a very lucrative market for the Portuguese. In the last couple of years for reasons unknown to us, Spain has stopped buying them but they are still grown by the Portuguese and as the market has seemed to dry up, they are leaving the fruit on the trees until they drop, then letting them rot on the ground. The more enterprising growers are now selling them on the roadside at €2.00 for five kilos.

We can now sit on the terrace of the Parador in Ayamonte in Spain, sipping a cool glass of beer and look over the hills to the river Guadiana which separates Spain from Portugal. The view is stunning, as we look with wonder at the beautiful architectural masterpiece of the suspension bridge, with its shiny steel struts supporting the road, which now gives us access to Spain and its vast array of supermarkets.

Years ago before the motorway was built and the bridge completed, the easiest way to get into Spain was to take the ferry from Villa Real to Ayamonte. This was a great boon to both the Spanish and Portuguese shoppers, as some items in Spain were cheaper than Portugal and vis-versa. So it was quite common to see ladies coming off the ferry on both sides of the river laden down their bargain purchases.

Now with the ferries almost redundant, the motorway links both countries and with the advent of the EU border controls being scrapped, the same thing happens with the shoppers but now the come in their cars by road.

It was the case that there was a great saving to be made by shopping in Spain. However, with increasing fuel prices and the equalisation of most prices in food costs, there is not much of a saving, even though fuel is still a tad cheaper in Spain; taking in to account the fuel price to get from Faro to Ayamonte and back, there is not much to be gained.

CHAPTER FIVE

Communication.

C ommunication? What a strange word to be used in the Algarve in 1984, as it was almost non-existent!

Telephones, postal services, the Internet, Sky, and television were either in their infancy or non-existent. So compared with the UK we were in the dark ages. If we wanted to make contact with friends we had made, we either had to call on them, leave a note under a stone at their front door, or go to Marias Deli and leave a message in their postal pigeon hole. Marias was also the centre for all contacts and local gossip. One of our friends who had lived in Africa all her adult life, was affectionately called the Gorgoe's radio service because once she knew of a bit of news, she would tell all with whom she came into contact. We understand that this was how the ex-pats kept in contact in Africa.

Another method we used was when we wanted to contact a friend in the next valley, we would shine a powerful torch at night at a pre-determined time and they would shine their torch from their house thereby knowing they wanted something and we would then call on each other. In the daytime we would wave large stripy pool umbrellas!

TELEPHONES

The telephone service was a nightmare. It would take up to five years to get a line after instigating the torturous procedure; queuing for hours at the Portuguese Telecom office with all the locals trying to get to the front of the line, then having to produce evidence of who we were, i.e. passport which would have to be photocopied ad nauseaum, address and proof of address in Portugal and England, details of bank accounts etc. Women were not allowed to apply without the permission of the husband, another signature, etc. etc. Then only to be told that there were no telephone wires in the area and would have to come back in five years and start the process again!

When Fearne and Philip Spark (see chapter on ex pats) decided to buy a house in the area, the deciding factor to buy was that it was connected to the telephone service!

So the only two ways we could make a telephone call was either to go to the Post Office in Santa Barbara, where they had pay phones or there was a small corner shop in Gorjoe's which had a phone. The shop literally was your original corner shop, a small mini market on the corner of the cross roads and was owned and run by a lady called Olivia, who did not speak a word of English. She had one of the only phones in the village and this was housed in a wooden booth inside the shop with a rickety old door with one small window. Inside, the black Bakelite phone was sitting on a wooden shelf. We would ask Olivier to connect the line and she would set a timer to start the operation. After the call she would stop the timer and tell us the cost. This all happened after we had to try and stop all the local women in the shop from chatting in order to get Olivier's attention, as this really was the local gossip centre.

Olivia's husband also ran the local builders merchants and on many occasions when we wanted building material (and her husband was usually out on a job) she would tell us to go to the yard, as it was always unlocked, open and take what we wanted. We would then ask Olivier what was the cost and invariably she would not know but would ask her husband. We would then keep calling into the shop to ask the price but she would still not know. This could go on for months and still not pay! What trust and honesty. This has nothing to do with telephones but interesting no less.

Eventually our line was installed and the service and reception was awful. Continually breaking down, especially in wet stormy weather or when a high builder's lorry came up the hill and snapped the cable.

POST

The postal service was not so bad but because we did not and still do not have a road name and official address. The post was left at Marias Deli in one of her of pigeon holes, just inside the entrance of the shop doorway. What a good way to entice people to come into the shop and buy her goods. She also had a large supply of stamps and English newspapers, which was a great hit with the ex-pats. 'Modern' metal post boxes are now placed in strategic areas around the village and have now replaced Marias pigeon holes.

The postage stamps bought at the post office were a revelation as they did not have any 'sticky' on the back. The postmaster would get out a jar of 'Gloy' glue with a long hairy brush and plaster the back of the stamp, then stick it onto the envelope. If we bought a pack of stamps we would also have to have some glue at home. Now most of the stamps have peel off backs, although only yesterday we bought stamps at the airport and the lady stuck them on with glue.

RADIO

The only radio service of course was Portuguese and we could not understand that, so we used a portable radio tuned permanently to the World Service, which had so many different wave bands for different times of the day, it was mind boggling. We would walk around the house trying to get a good signal with the radio pressed to the ear in order to hear it properly!

INTERNET

The internet was not invented in 1984, so there was no question of whether it was good or bad or indifferent, it just was not there. When eventually Portugal Telecom got up to speed with it, they did not have a clue how to make it work. Initially they introduced dial up internet as we did in the UK and this was a disaster. Not only was there no way of finding out how to get connected, when we did, it was even slower than the UK system and was always disconnecting. Eventually they advertised Sapo, which was their version of Broadband but of course this did not work either. Sure, they would sell us a system, but after purchasing the appropriate software and installing it on the computer, it also would not work. On contacting PT they then informed us that there were too many people wanting the service in our area so the signal was too weak. So, then having the service cancelled they continued to charge us the monthly fee for the next four years!

Not knowing that we were still connected and did not pay for the original software, the first we knew about it was when we received a solicitor's letter threatening to take us to court for non-payment of €25.00, even though we had continued to pay for a service we had not had for four years!

TV

We now have a version of Sky TV, which, after a lot of expense and many visits by the engineer, works very well but in extreme wet and windy weather the picture will break up. So after twenty seven years we have been dragged screaming into the twenty first century.

ROADS

Communication by road was fraught with dangers. There were no motorways to take us along the length of the Algarve, only the EN 125 single carriageway road. It was badly designed and littered with accident spots. It was quite common to see three cars overtaking each other on a blind right hand bend, with the appropriate high death rate. It had the reputation of being the most dangerous road in Europe. When a local vicar was asked by a parishioner how he should pray, the vicar said go and drive on the EN125!! Now thanks to EU money, we have a two/three lane motorway running the length of the Algarve and we all feel a lot safer driving.

Now in order to really 'cock things up' the government is imposing tolls on all motorways, (which will help ruin the already struggling tourist industry) including the tourist busy motorway, Via Infanta, which was built to replace the EN125; so we expect to see most traffic back on the EN125 again, as most locals will not pay to drive on the motorway, nor will we. They have just started to erect the gantries which will support the cameras which register vehicles for the tolls and we are now told that they cannot use the system because its use has not been agreed by parliament. We have to wait until a new government is formed in June 2011, and if the opposition party is elected it is rumoured they will scrap the system, with the resulting waste of millions of taxpayers Euros.

Like the whole world over, a typical crazy situation created by a bunch of incompetent politicians, attempting to run the country into bankruptcy. They get the country into debt and then the people have to pay more exorbitant taxes to get them out of the mess. Portugal now has to borrow 78 billion Euros from the EU as a bail out, (of which the UK owes eight billion as their contribution) and if they do not get their finances under control, the country will be in administration run by Brussels!

ELECTRICITY

Well! What can we say about the EDP Electricity Company. The weirdest situation, where they use smoke and mirrors to confuse us all in the strangest commercial system we have ever seen. When having the new house built in '84 it was a revelation when it came to the electricity supply. We were given what is laughingly called a 'builders supply' connected to the site, this meant enough electricity to run an electric cement mixer and a light bulb! The wires appeared from nowhere and we cannot remember whether there was a meter or not. 'Full' electricity would not be laid onto the house until a 'habitation licence' was issued by the council, after they had inspected the building and deemed it 'habitable' Of course that was when they decided to visit the site in their own time. Councils seem to be the same all over the world. Slow! So we had to move into the house using only the builder's supply which would hardly run a kettle and cooker. Unbeknown to us, this kept the builder happy, as they would not get their final payment for the house if there was no electric laid on. So having the meagre builders supply meant they got their final payment.

On a couple of occasions when returning to the house from the UK we found a new electricity cable connected to one of our outside power points, disappearing out of our plot and over the hills. Tracing the cable for some half a kilometre, we found another builder using our electricity to run his new house building site! So we turned off our power supply, disconnected the lead and waited for the result. Sure enough in the afternoon the builder's agent came to see why their latest client was without power. He explained that his client was leaving for the UK the next day and was desperate to have power for bathing cooking etc. and could we please reconnect for the next twenty four hours. Of course we knew that what he wanted was for the client to have power until they went home, so that he could receive his final payment for the construction of the house!

As they had stolen our electricity as far as we knew for some weeks or maybe months, we were somewhat annoyed to say the least, so we said in no way could they steal any more of our power. There was no offer of compensation for the power used, nor an apology for the illegal connection to our cables. The agent tried everything to persuade us to reconnect but Fay was so incensed that she sent him off with a flea in his ear and a boot up his bum. Whether he got his final payment we never knew.

On another occasion we returned from the UK to find a cable connected to our pool pump running to a building site adjacent to our house and the builders were running their crane and cement mixer from our power! This tale does not have much to do with our electricity story but an interesting ditty no less!

Now the situation has changed completely. When a plot of land gets planning permission, the electricity is connected to the site with full power and a meter is housed in a brick pillar which is permanent. This has led to the brick pillar being incorporated into wide sweeping curved entrance walls, ending in black wrought iron gates to the drive entrance. Some of these are electrically operated and seems to be the latest must have status symbol.

So, back to the EDP. Not being technically minded, we understood that we have 'three faze' electricity whatever that is, and finally connected through a meter. However, in the UK we have electricity laid on to our homes and we pay for as much power as we use. Not in Portugal. We have the choice of 10, 15, 20, 25, or 30 amps, each amount of amps costing more for the power. If 10 amps are agreed, then every time we tried to use more than 10 amps power, then the supply would fail! So to run normal household appliances with heating etc. one must pay the biggest price of 30 amps, on the basis that if we can afford all those appliances, we must be wealthy and therefore can afford to pay more, thereby subsidising those poorer people who could not afford more than 10amps!

We had additional problems in wet and stormy weather when for some reason the electricity would 'surge' and burn out many appliances such as pool pumps, fridges, televisions etc. Also main fuses would blow and cut off the juice. The good news was that EDP were always, and still are, very fast in making the repairs and would pay for these appliances to be replaced at no cost to the customer. Now in 2011 we rarely have these problems as the current seems much more stable.

It is our view that many of the English new comers to the Algarve would not have bought homes here if they had to have the services, (or lack of them) that we had in the beginning.

CHAPTER SIX

Air travel

J udith Chalmers the TV personality, presented a travel programme in the 70s called 'Wish You Were Here' and one of the most popular, was an edition about Vale Do Lobo in the Algarve, where we believe she had a holiday home. This was one of the most watched and really put the area on the map for many holidaymakers. At this time the package holiday business was just starting to become the norm with European destinations and people flocked to the Algarve as a result of the programme. In addition to the package deals, there were also scheduled flights to Faro.

We used to lie sunbathing on the hot sand in the summer near Vale Do Lobo (where the sand was so hot we had to wear sand shoes on our feet to stop them burning) and watch the aircraft make their final approach to the airport. Then there were not that many flights each hour but now we can be on the same beach and on some days there is around five or six aeroplanes landing each hour.

The cost of a schedule air flight on British Airways in 1984 was around £500.00 return and upwards for two people in cattle class and there was no way we could buy a one way ticket. If that was required, one had to buy a return ticket, then not take the return flight, thereby wasting £250.00! Now we can book a return flight for as little as €45.00 and in addition can arrange a one way flight. Wow! How times have changed.

There was a travel scam going on where somebody had a return flight that they did not want to use and a friend wanted to travel on the ticket. They would both turn up at the airport and book in the official ticket holder at the departure desk, the person with the ticket would then sell it to the friend and the friend would go through to departures and board the plane with no questions asked!!

As scheduled flights were so expensive and packaged deals were in their infancy; way back in the 1950s/60s there was an organisation formed called the Upminster Travel Club and was the first organisation to arrange charter flights to European destinations. Up to this point in time, airlines mostly flew schedule flights with very high fixed prices. The Club got together groups of likeminded people who wished to have cheaper flights and they hired and filled an aircraft for charter. This fare also had to include accommodation, even if only a dormitory (which was normally a bit of a dump) so nobody ever used these and would book additional hotels separately. Therefore they would get the flight and accommodation at a much reduced price because they negotiated directly with the airline. Hence the charter business took off, if you will excuse the pun! The rest is history. Now people can get a one way flight for as little as £25.00 and then complain that they have to pay additional costs for heavy luggage. However, the low cost airlines are increasingly trying to make more money from existing customers and are reducing the physical size of hand luggage, to try to get more into the hold thereby charging additional fees for overweight and oversized baggage. At these new low prices who can blame them?

The new cheaper airlines such as Flybe, Ryan Air, Easy Jet, etc. knocked seven bells out of the scheduled airlines and we all rejoiced at the low costs and flexibility of booking and seating arrangements, even if we did get a British Rail type tired stale sandwich thrown at us as 'lunch'; but if we want cheap flights, the profit needs to come from somewhere.

On many occasions when flying to and from the UK with British Airways, we would ask the pilot if we could sit in the cockpit and watch the landing or take off and this we did many times. In addition during the flight, there would be queues of children and mums and dads waiting to go on the flight deck, talk to the pilots and watch the flight progress. Things have now changed dramatically and are a lot different since the Twin Towers terrorist attack in the USA. Not only are we subjected to strip searches, ex ray machines checking our luggage, and not allowed to carry on liquids, the pilots are locked in the cockpit and the cabin crew are only allowed in, after they have entered a password into the door keypad. Recently a pilot was stopped at the security scanner after having his flight bag X rayed and a nail clipper was confiscated. He asked the security man if he thought he might clip his co-pilot to death! Prior to these restrictions, on one such flight we were both in the cockpit for a landing. There was no sophisticated landing technology at Faro airport and landing was done by pilot sight only, on a clear day. The ground control tower came through on the radio and said we were OK to land but there were four other aircraft to land before us. Both pilots then had to find the other four by sight, get in the queue and watch and wait for them to land. They could only see three and asked us to look out of the windows to see if we could see the fourth. We located the fourth and prepared to land. Were we sweating!

Faro airport has been modernised and updated so many times, (airports are a bit like Disney World, they will never be finished) it is now a very sophisticated international airport with all mod cons, is frenetically busy and now has some thirty plus, check in desks. There are many snack bars and shops, none of which were there when we first travelled. There are large long and short term car parks, very well organised and relatively low cost compared with the UK. A typical one week stay in the long term park at Faro is around €57.00, in the UK £80.00. There is now a company offering off site airport parking at much lower rates and they will take you to the airport and pick up on your return.

Many bookings are computerised and we can now book flights, reserve seats and print boarding cards on the internet from the comfort of our own home. This means that if we do not have hold luggage we do not have to queue to book in. What incredible progress from 1984. Not only that, on the internet we can track which airport the aircraft is taking off from, whether it is taxying or just taken off and watch the progress of the flight flying all the way to its destination.

On one occasion we had to go back to the UK in great haste but could not get a flight from Faro as they were all full, so we drove in our own car to Lisbon to catch a flight from there. We parked the car in the long term car park (which is only a short walk from the terminal) in a parking spot almost under a fly-over in the shade, which we thought would be out of the sun and keep it cool for our return. When we flew back to Lisbon and went to pick up the car, it had gone from the spot where we left it and was parked some fifty meters away. How it got moved is a mystery, it was locked, with the alarm set and was unmarked!

Relatively speaking flight delays are a thing of the past and the majority of flights arrive on time, we understand this is due to more sophisticated computerised traffic control. In earlier days a two to three hour delay was seen as normal. One flight we took from Manchester, was delayed for twelve hours.

Our daughter who was fifteen at the time, took a BA flight on her own from Gatwick, which was twenty eight hours late! When she arrived at Gorjoe's at five o clock in the morning, the taxi driver could not find our house and asked a local five year old boy for the directions. He climbed into the taxi and gave directions all the way to the house. What was a five year old doing out on his own at that time of the day? We later found out his name was Rodrigo, who is now a mature adult and drives the dreaded Piagio. On the Manchester twelve hour delay flight, we were flying with Orion Air which was a lovely airline with which to fly, unfortunately due to the fierce competition it is now no more. However, due to the long delay the pilot and cabin crew were so apologetic, that once we were in the air they threw open the bar including Champagne and everything was free. There were only thirty four people on board and by the end of the flight were all a bit tipsy to say the least. When we landed, nobody wanted to get off as we were all having such a good party. The Captain and First Officer came out to have a chat for a while and in the end they said that we must disembark as they had get ready for the return flight!

What a super way to end this chapter!

CHAPTER SEVEN

Cars, vehicles and trains.

W here do we start to describe the comparison of cars within the UK and the Algarve in 1984, as the subject is so huge. So let's start with the first time we arrived at the airport. We had pre-booked a car from the UK via one of the large rental companies, probably Hertz, as they were one of the largest and well known in the world. The options were pretty limited; as Henry Ford said 'You can have any colour you like as long as it is black' our fantastic choice for our budget was a Mini or a Mini! We had expected to drive it away from the airport but of course it was not ready and we had to have a taxi to the rented Villa, with the promise that the car would be delivered to our Villa the next day, which it was. Big surprise!

The car was in reasonable condition (which is more than we could say for its condition when we returned it, but more of that later) and quite a high mileage. We thought that as we were a bit hard up we should only hire a cheap Mini, and thought there would be hundreds of other makes for hire and many types of cars to choose from. Oh no, as far as memory goes it was a Mini or nothing. Our first trip out was a revelation, there were so few cars on the road and those we saw were mostly very old and in shabby condition. In the UK we drove a small BMW and we felt that had we driven from England to use it in Portugal we would have been very conspicuous and out of place. There were quite a few very old Mercedes, shabby Renaults and it was quite common to see tractors driven by country people, with the wife sitting in the bucket attached to the back. Other small vehicles in abundance were the three wheeled Piagio vans and open trucks with a tiny two stroke engine which did 0 to 60kph in two days!

Anyhow, the Mini served us well for the duration of the holiday, until one evening returning to the villa after a most delicious meal and too much vino, we parked the car on the sloping gravel drive and went to bed. In the morning we found the car had rolled across the drive and hit a dry stone wall. Of course this happens if one fails to put on the handbrake when Brahms and List! The hire company was not overjoyed when we returned it at the end of the week.

The tradesmen's lorries from small to quite large articulated jobbies were disasters waiting to happen. Overloaded, badly maintained, some travelling crabwise and many not taxed or insured, they were to be avoided at all cost. In the last fifteen years the MOT test has been introduced and this has taken most of the rogues off the road, in addition the police have stepped up their spot inspections, especially on trade vehicles and the situation has improved significantly. Over the years motorcycles have varied from 50cc mopeds to 500 cc maxi scooters and thundering great two litre four cylinder giants capable of well over 180 klms per hour, with the inevitable death rate in young men. In 1984 the most common to be seen were small 150 cc motorcycle's ridden by elderly country gentlemen with an orange box tied onto the back carrier with string, used for carrying all sorts of goods. Overloaded with shopping, dogs, bales of hay and ladies, mostly carried very precariously on the rear and sometimes in addition, a child on the petrol tank; we were sure to give them a very wide berth when overtaking. Crash helmets are required by law but our macho men not wishing to be seen to be wimp's, leave then undone, with the chinstraps flying in the wind. It is very common to see a baseball cap worn under the helmet with the peak sticking out, so when the helmet is taken off, the cap covers the bald head!

In July every year, the Moto Club of Faro organises a three day biker's weekend festival in the open ground near Faro airport and bikers from around the world assemble and camp for a great jamboree. The numbers vary from 28,000 to 40,000 with all types of machines including our country gentlemen with the orange box on the back of the bike. Rock groups pound away until the late hours with motorcycle memorabilia stalls, strip shows and food stalls; it is quite a wonderful event. You will never have seen in your life so many bald heads and tattoo's in one place and that's only the women! On the last Sunday of the festival, there is a parade and final dispersal of the bikes from the camp site, riding into and around Faro with all the noise and carnival atmosphere expected; girls in bikinis and tattoos standing on the backs of bikes taking video's and photo's, phew! Locals and holidaymakers line the route cheering and waving them on. It is quite a spectacle.

Most gipsies were travelling in the traditional horse and cart with all goods, chattels and many children loaded in and around the cart. Nowadays this is less of a sight as they tend to drive the Piagio's and the horse and cart becomes less common, although there are still many around. Recently when visiting a Mercedes car showroom there was a Gipsy family complete with mum, dad, loads of kids, grandma and granddad, purchasing a brand new Mercedes 15cwt van. Much to the disgust of the salesman and the rest of the showroom staff, as the noise and odour was something to behold! They did the deal in double quick time and ushered them out tout-suite, de-odourising the showroom as they went. Where they got the money for such an expensive purchase we leave to the imagination.

So, having bought the villa and bent the hire car, we thought we should save shed loads of money by buying a small cheap car, rather than renting every time we came on holiday. The restaurant we had dined at prior to the handbrake debacle (as mentioned earlier) was called Lady Susan's in Faro, owned by an English couple we also mentioned earlier. We became firm friends with them and still socialise with them to this day. When we were in England we posed the question (by snail mail letter) of buying a car and they said they would research the market ready for the next time we came out to Portugal. Sure enough within a few months they had found a car, guess what, a Mini. Ug! They arranged for us to see it on our next trip and full of anticipation we met them in Faro at the appointed time the owner had arranged. You guessed it, nobody turned up; so after waiting a respectable time we gave up and went for another boozy lunch. Discussing the situation over the meal we said that we had seen a nice car that we fancied in the local Faro Citroen dealership. A Mehari Jeep, a plastic version of the world famous 2CV.

As we had lost out the Mini, which was a relief, we asked Susan and Robert to come with us to the dealer and talk the talk in Portuguese with the sales people. As it happened, the salesman turned out to be one of the Lady Susan's regular customers, a gent called George Baptista, (bit of a ladies man by all accounts) who Robert knew quite well. The car we lusted after was a brand new plastic jeep version of the Citroen called a Mehari Azure, with a two cylinder air cooled 600cc engine. Having loved quirky cars all our life, this suited our needs and our new to be lifestyle in the Algarve. Cheap to run, and the back seat could be take out and could be converted into a small truck, open on all sides and with a sun roof for the wonderful sunny weather.

The price was around £3000.00, was one of the last ones manufactured as it was being discontinued, and was lovely! It was white with a blue roof and go faster stripes. We asked George if he would accept payment by credit card which he said was not allowed. So how about an English cheque? No, as it could bounce. Damm it, we were desperate for the car to use straight away, rather than hiring another rented car for the next two weeks. Then George asked Robert if he would guarantee the cheque and to our surprise he agreed, which is pretty amazing really, as we were almost strangers to him. George agreed and the deal was done. He asked when we wanted the car and we said **now** and wanted to drive it out of the showroom. He said this was not possible, the cheque needs to be cleared, the car needed pre-delivery checks and a thorough clean.

We said this did not matter to us and to our amazement he agreed and said he would send all the necessary papers and the Liverette (log book) on to our Portuguese address as soon as it was completed from Lisbon.

We drove out of the showroom and off to our new house with grins like two Cheshire Cats, thinking that this situation would never have been allowed in the UK. We did not give a thought about road tax (this was to bite us in the bum some seven years later) although George did insist that we insured the car through Citroen; which we did.

In 1991 we were again in Lady Susan's restaurant, another boozy dinner, and Robert reminded us that it was the law in Portugal that we must carry the original Liverette with us in the car at all times, no copies allowed. The Police were, and are now very hot on these issues and the fines for non-compliance are very heavy. Liverette, Liverette we asked what is that? After Robert's explanation the penny dropped, George had forgotten to send it to us and we had also forgotten all about it as we had only spent a few weeks each year in Portugal. We hot footed it back to Citroen and told George and he went white! Panic written all over his face, he apologised profusely and immediately put the administration wheels into action and we received the dammed thing in the post a few weeks later.

Not only had we no log book, and as we were not in the country very often, we had forgotten to pay the road taxes for all those years! Although the tax is only about €5.00 a year it was still illegal. So for seven years we had driven illegally and also not been stopped by the Police in one of their frequent road checks! Last year we were stopped three times! We think the police are now paid commission on the fines levied.

As we had defaulted on the road tax, we had to go to the Financa's to tax the car and pay the appropriate fine. This was a very strange experience, a bit like the telephone procedure. Queue up for around two hours to reach the front of the queue, to be confronted by a hatchet face old 'cap and a book of tickets' clerk behind a glass panel, only to be told in Portuguese that we did not have the appropriate form and would have to queue up at the next counter, to buy the form for ten cents from another equally unhelpful council jobsworth. By the time we had bought the form and filled it in, we had lost our place in the queue and we had to start again! Now the procedure is so much simpler. The Financa's send a reminder a month before the car tax is due and we take it to the local post office and pay for it in cash. It seems that civil servants are the same the world over, they are neither civil or servants! Having said that, in the past twenty seven years, the council staff have become so much more helpful.

Not wishing to bore the reader but it is worth telling the following tale. Having had the car MOT tested ever since the test was introduced, it had passed without any problems every year. Until three years ago some officious tester decided that the chassis number was illegible, illegal and refused to pass it. At one point we were accused of stealing the chassis and would be taken to court! To cut a very long boring story short, it was off the road for two years and due to the ridiculous bureaucracy cost £700.00 in administration fees to put right. Went in for its final test and because the chassis number was now legal it passed, with two split tyres!!! No further comment is required.

The Mehari is now twenty six years old, in fantastic condition, has only covered 59,000 klms and as they are not in production anymore has become a collector's item. We were recently offered the price we paid for it when it was new but it is not for sale! Unless somebody offers us a million! Everything has its price!

Our Citroen Mehari

Now in 2010, the populace are much more affluent and hire purchase has been introduced for some years, so much newer cars are on the road and more up market models seem commonplace. Mercedes, BMW, Audi and the occasional Bentley and Roller are in evidence. Rumour has it that the government encouraged the Portuguese to take out hire purchase for cars on very advantageous terms but due to the high cost of repayments, many have defaulted on the payments, the cars are being snatched back and put on the used car market, which is now flooded with expensive used cars.

The Portuguese have now fallen in love with the motor car and need to learn how to drive them safely. The favourite pastime at present is to drive like the Devil is after them, 95% drive like the wind and tailgate every vehicle they find on the road, in order to scare the driver into letting them pass. The other 5% normally wear a peaked flat hat and drive like a snail and they are always in front of us!

As it was in 1984, folks will still stop in the middle of a country road when passing a friend in another car, wind down the window and will have a chat, oblivious of any queue piling up behind the them. But this is all part of the charm of the Algarve.

One of the greatest joys of travelling on the roads is that there is so little traffic, sometimes on a Sunday we can travel for miles and miles without seeing another vehicle. The really splendid news is that we are increasingly having more dual carriageway roads built around the area and many traffic lights are being replaced with roundabouts. This has eased some of the problems with delays at lights. One particular set at Quattro Stradas near Almancil, led to enormous delays and now there is a new roundabout there is no delay.

The new roundabouts being built are beautifully designed and maintained, either landscaped with trees shrubs and flowers or have a sculpted theme. The Loul'e one has a fountain playing into the centre with two dancing sculpting's atop an enormous stone circle with the figure of an accordionist playing at the bottom of an artificial pond.

Other roundabouts are beautifully manicured with lawns, trees and shrubs and are very well maintained. The funniest situation happened at a roundabout near the Continente Supermarket in Loul'e, where again a nicely built roundabout structure planted with old gnarled olive trees and covered in multi-coloured gravel was built. Around the circumference there was a motorway type crash barrier; it was crashed into so many times by lorries and cars and subsequently repaired, the council dismantled it permanently!

One of the nicest trips to make in the early days was to take the train to Lisbon. The diesel train left from Loul'e station, which incidentally is nowhere near Loul'e but some eight kilometres away, and would leave about 07.00. The first class ticket was £18.00 for two people which included a reserved seat. The train was fast, express all the way, air conditioned, comfortable, clean and had a restaurant car for snacks and meals. The white suited waiter service was first class, the meals were cheap and as usual in Portugal good value for money. The fascinating part of the three and a half hour trip was the arrival at the station, which was the end of the line. The train pulled into the joint train and ferry terminal on the opposite side of Lisbon, across the Tagus River. Not having done the journey before, we did not realise that the train ticket included the cost of the ferry crossing to Lisbon. There we stood, not knowing where to go to catch the ferry, so the only thing to do was to follow the crowd, which was extremely large, and hope for the best.

The ferry was an experience in itself, quite old but in good condition it was absolutely jam packed with all sorts of people of all nationalities and ages. Ladies going to do the town for the day, business people, students, teenagers, children, housewives with shopping bags, suitcases and travel bags everywhere. The noise of people chatting away was almost deafening, a real taste of all levels of Portuguese life in miniature. The river crossing took around twenty minutes and on docking at the other side, it was only a short walk to the underground station to the centre of Lisbon. This was a really interesting, unusual trip and a jolly good day out.

The latest addition to the rail journey is that the whole line has now been electrified, together with updated rails, trains and carriages and the journey time is significantly shorter. In addition the ferry is no more part of the rail trip and the train now crosses a bridge and terminates in Lisbon, which is a much more efficient route but of course, not as much fun.

CHAPTER EIGHT

Ex-Pats

The majority of people we have met who have moved to the Algarve recently call themselves 'ex pats' but of course in the true sense of the word they are not. They are people who have bought a home abroad and possibly still maintain a home in the UK and travel backwards and forwards. Our understanding of true ex-patriot's, are those people who left England in their youth and went to work abroad for the majority of their working life.

We have met many real ex-pats in our time in the Algarve and they are certainly a different and dying breed to those described above. They normally are tough, resilient, self-motivated, positive, and intelligent people who have worked in foreign lands building and managing businesses for themselves or their companies, in very difficult and sometimes hazardous environments. They worked in places like Africa, the Sudan, Hong Kong, South America, India, Arabia, Singapore, Ceylon etc.

In their working lives they represented their companies overseas, because it was very difficult to do business in ways other than being based in the countries; thereby helping the locals to make business and administration systems work effectively. In those days air travel was in its infancy and other forms of travel took ages to get anywhere in the world, so one of the only options was to live and work permanently in the country. Now air travel being so fast and cheap, executives can leap on a plane at a moment's notice and be back for the weekend without necessarily being permanently based overseas.

We have met and become firm friends with many of the real ex-pats who have retired to Portugal, most of whom never lived their adult life in the UK and some who were born abroad to parents who were also ex-pats. It is interesting to mention a few of these people to outline the varied and challenging career's they pursued.

Dick Jones

Dick Jones (and his wife Sheena who has now died) moved to the Algarve some twenty five years ago, leaving their three adult offspring in the UK. Dick was a Marketing Director of a well-known Multinational Company and worked in Kenya, Brazil, Nigeria, Sudan, Hong Kong and Indonesia. Originally in the army, Dick spent his life travelling around the world with his wife and children, all of whom were schooled in the UK. As they were growing up, he only saw them in school holidays. Dick and Sheena loved their unusual and varied life abroad, had a holiday home in Livramento, Portugal and subsequently retired there. Through his travels he took a menagerie of animals with him including two dogs and two parrots, a Blue Fronted Amazon called Henry and an African Grey called

Percy, who talks non-stop, swears like a trooper and is forty year's old. Henry was stolen during a break in at Dick's house. Percy has had three heart attacks and is still going strong. We looked after Percy for two weeks while Dick was on holiday and he had one of his heart attacks whilst in our care. He squawked very loudly, fell of his perch, laid on the bottom of his cage moaning, twitching and hanging on to his perch with one leg, then recovered within the hour! On asking Dick what we should have done with him had he died, he said we should have put him in the freezer until he returned from holiday and he would deal with the corpse at a later date. Since living in Portugal Dick has acquired three dozen tumbling doves, dozens of foreign finches and loads of budgerigars which breed profusely. One of his dogs died of old age and the other went blind, fell in the swimming pool and drowned!

Philip and Fearne Spark.

They are now in their late seventies are still going strong, play three games of golf every week, swim every day, summer and winter and are as fit as fleas. Their brains are as sharp as razors and they regularly play Bridge with other retiree's. Fearne was born in Ceylon and swam for England in the 1956 Olympic Games. Phil was in his late teens, commuting into London every day and decided that the boredom of this lifestyle was not for him, so he upped sticks, moved out of the UK and at age twenty one, was running a rubber plantation in Malaya responsible for three thousand employees.

He spent years traveling and working around the world including the USA, the Far East, Africa and South America and Peru, ending up as one of the Chief Executives of an Inchcape Company overseas running the operation and trouble shooting for them. They have two grown up children, one in the UK manufacturing and selling toys and the other living in South Africa.

Pat and Tony Clifford.

Tony was born on a farm in Africa and his father was killed in the second world war, leaving him, his brother and sisters and his mother, who was very competent, to run a very large ranch. He would often be heard to say when confronting a difficult problem, 'you think that is difficult, you should see my mum strip down a tractor'! Pat was born in the UK, trained as a secretary and decided at the age of twenty one she would go to Africa to find a job. She told her parents of her plans and they not believing she would go said, 'yes dear off you go' so to their amazement she did. She met and married Tony soon after her arrival.

For all of their married life they ran coffee farms for a French company, which moved them around to different or new farms every five or six years. They could employ as many as three thousand Africans when the coffee crop was being harvested. Tony is six foot five, big with it and by all accounts looked magnificent riding around the farm on a horse, complete with shorts, bushman's hat and rifle. That is Tony, not the horse! He also used a motorcycle to get from place to place. He is a bit of a 'Crocodile Dundee' sort of guy, tough, resourceful, inventive and could cope with any situation which came his way. One day we needed a new leather washer for a valve in our systerna pipework system, so hotfooted round to Tony's house, knowing that he would have something that would suffice. He took us into his workshop which was equipped well enough to maintain a battleship and after rooting around for a bit he found a large piece of leather and promptly fashioned a washer for our needs. Asking him what type of leather he used, he said without drawing breath, it's an elephant's ear! This could only happen with a chap like Tony.

He also does not suffer fools gladly and a good guy to have around in a crisis. He is the sort of guy you would not mind being marooned with on a dessert island, as he would know exactly how to survive.

Pat and Tony went on many Safaris in the bush and whilst on one, Tony went down to the river to have a swim and bathe. As he entered the water he aroused a sleeping Buffalo and it attacked and gored him very badly. Being miles from anywhere, he had to be rushed to the nearest hospital where he nearly died of gangrene. This experience left him with a very badly scarred leg. On another occasion, one of the farm bitches was on heat and when this happened he would put the dog into a large wooden box which was fixed at high level in a tree where the other dogs could not reach. They called it the hot dog box! When he went to lift the dog into the box it bit one of his fingers which had to be amputated.

Just to demonstrate how primitive things were in the early days in the Algarve, Pat and Tony did not have electricity laid on to their house, so they had a generator for power. At night when they got into bed, they had a length of string running from the bedroom, out through the window, passing through many pulleys and the other end was connected to the 'off' switch on the generator; when they were ready to go to sleep, they would pull the string to turn of the generator!

Pat is mentally and physically tough, helped with the farm, managed the house and the servants, she was general help, counsellor and nurse to the African staff and an all-round good egg. She was chair lady of the Nairobi Women's League and has spent all her life helping other people have a good life. She has always done this at the expense of her own health and wellbeing, whilst bringing up two boys, who like most settlers children were educated in the UK. One now runs his own metal/fabrication business in the UK and the other is an accountant to a Charity in London.

When she and Tony retired and moved to the Algarve, she continued her good works being a prison visitor and hospital assistant, helping English people understand the hospital systems and Portuguese language. She is Church Warden and a pillar of the local Anglican Church of St Luke's and enriches so many people's lives with her good works. On 21st April 2011 she was presented to the Queen in Westminster Abbey and received the Maundy Money for her efforts in the Church in the Algarve. In later years Tony has had terrible problems with his feet and now in his mid-seventies is very immobile and cannot get around easily.

After all those years growing coffee in Africa, they do not drink coffee!

Anne and Gerald Plumer.

Gerald was a Captain in the English Navy and towards the end of his career was the British Naval Attaché to Lisbon. Again, like most real ex-pats, had lived and worked all over the world. They built a house opposite ours in Gorjoe's and we met them and most of the others mentioned in this chapter at their house party, some twenty years ago. We do not know as much about them, as they were the first of our friends to die. Nevertheless he was great company with a wealth of Navy stories from around the world. One of the workmen was working in our house, saw the name Plumer on Gerald's gate opposite us and said, Gor blimey guvnor' the plumbers must be really wealthy around here!

Sally and Jeremy Bull.

Jeremy left the UK with his parents when he was eighteen months old and they moved to South Africa. When he was twelve years old he returned to school in England and at sixteen was farming in Yorkshire. He then immigrated to Rhodesia for five years. Finally he settled in Portugal. He joined Taylors Port wine company and became their most competent Port Wine expert, which he did for over twenty five years. We call him 'Chip' as his humour is as dry as a Chip Dry Port. He has an amazing ability to taste a Port from almost anywhere and will tell us which Port House it comes from and most time can state the year it was bottled. We often try to catch him out with a blind tasting of an unusual Port and most times he will get it right. Now in his very late seventies has just started to renovate a small sailing yacht, and with Sally, tows it down to Faro and spends a large part of the summer sailing around the Algarve coast.

Sally is a very warm and dear friend, great fun and has positive and light hearted attitude to life. She has run her own jam making and greetings card business and has had some serious illness lately with which she dealt with great gusto, with a positive attitude. She is a great cook and hostess and fun to be around.

Ann and Paul Lucas.

Paul took a job as Training Manager for the HSBC Bank and lived around the world with Ann for many years. They had tours of duty in Hong Kong where they lived in Apartment's for seven years, spent three winters in Buffalo (where they shuffled down to) in New York State; which was very cold and here they lived in a company house.

In Singapore and Saudi they lived in multi-national compounds but they were both detached houses with private access. The multi-cultural community living was very useful for bridging cultural differences and was a great excuse for celebrating non English festivals e.g. Diwali and they could dress accordingly. In Saudi, Ann was not allowed to go out of the compound without being covered in a black robe down to the floor, called an Abaya, together with a black headscarf but was allowed to show her face. She was also not allowed to wear a crucifix or own a Bible, as being found with these would either incur a sentence in prison or deportation post haste. Because she is a woman she was also not allowed to drive and had to be chauffeured around.

One of Paul's colleagues was told to take a posting to Saudi and as he was a committed Christian and wanted to take his Bible with him, which was not allowed, he had to resign!

As with most ex-pats, they have travelled and lived around the world and have a fascinating fund of interesting stories to tell.

They are very interesting, great fun and always in demand at Algarve dinner parties.

Jilly and Derek Lister

Derek moved to Portugal from the UK and owned and managed a textile business in Oporto. He then ran this operation until he retired.

He met Jilly when she was on stage in a dancing Show, they had a whirlwind romance and soon married; a real love match. He and Jilly bought a forty five foot yacht which they sailed from Greece, through the Mediterranean seas to Portugal, eventually mooring and living at Villamoura. They then spent a large proportion of their retired life sailing the local seas. Derek had a master mariner's licence which enabled him to sail ships up to many thousands of tons, so was a very able seaman. Jilly is an exceptionally strong swimmer and if the propeller got fouled, thought nothing of diving over the side and freeing the screw. Derek did a lot of the maintenance on the boat in the dry dock and one day whilst attending to a high part of the boat fell and damaged his back very badly. This led to a lot of ill health later in his life. Eventually as he was dying, his favourite phrase was 'old age and ill health is not for cissys' He had a great sense of humour and a very dear chum.

Jilly spent most of her unmarried life as a hoofer, showgirl dancer and straight gal for Tommy Trinder. She would feed him the lines and he would deliver the gag and get the laughs. We have never met such an extrovert, hilarious and off the wall lady in all of our days. She danced herself around most of the flesh spots of the world and has a fund of amazing and funny stories of what she did and experienced in the world of show business. She drinks like a fish and is an absolute riot at a dinner party. Jilly is much loved, is now a widow, still very sought after as a dinner guest and wows us all with her extrovert nature and zest for life.

She and Derek had a very close, and at times volatile and fiery relationship which boiled to a head one liquid lunch on our sun terrace. Derek had a very fine singing voice and Jilly was feeding him the words of the 'Beatles Yesterday' love song and Derek was singing them, together with the assembled lunch guests all at all full throttle, as shown in the above photograph.

When it was time for them to leave, they were both well sozzled. As usual in the heat, Jilly was wearing a bikini top and bottom which only just covered all her bits, with a see through flimsy sarong covering the lower regions, looked voluptuous and fabulous. When they drove into Loul'e, the drink and the heat had got to them and they had a flaming row in the car. Things are a bit hazy at this point as we were not there but either Derek stopped the car and threw her out in the street or Jilly got out. Derek drove of at great speed and left Jilly half-dressed in the middle of the very crowded street. She then had to walk through the town to find a taxi to take her home, much to the amazed stares of the crowds!

All of the above people are real ex-pats in the true sense of the word. The other newcomers to the Algarve, who call themselves ex-pats, cannot generally compare with those described above. These people in earlier days may have bought homes in the Spanish Costa's, had Spain not treated their immigrants so badly, knocking their houses down and building roads through them for very spurious reasons. So around six years ago a lot of them moved to Portugal because the pound was very strong against the Euro and having sold property in the UK could get a good financial deal on a Portuguese property. They received much better treatment and respect from the Portuguese. Who can blame them!

CHAPTER NINE

Weather

I t is now March 2011 and we are flying into the approach to Faro airport on an El Cheapo Monarch Airbus. This would normally take ten minutes after the pilot has told the crew to take their seats. Twenty minutes later we are still in the air and flying over the sea, with the cabin crew looking a bit anxious and saying the approach does not normally take this amount of time. As we came into land the reason became clear, we were landing in the most atrocious rainstorm and the pilot was obviously waiting for a break in the weather in order to land safely.

As we ran down the aircraft steps to catch the transfer bus and getting soaked in the process, we looked a very bedraggled group of travellers, some dressed in shorts, straw hats and tee shirts with I LOVE THE ALGARVE emblazoned on the front. The comments from some of the group with very glum faces were 'we came here for the Sun' and 'we did not expect it to rain in Portugal' It never ceases to amaze us that when people leave the gloomy English weather to go to anywhere in the world, they expect the weather to be sunny and warm! You definitely won't find the following words about the weather in any of the Portuguese travel or tourist books. The Algarve certainly does have its share of bad wet weather during the winter months between November and March/April, which is why the countryside is so green. A friend of ours, who has lived here for over twenty five years, calls Portugal a damp country with a hot sun. The winters can be very cold and down to minus two degrees in some frost pockets.

During our time here we have experienced really horrid weather, with thunder storms and torrential rain where our hillside road looked more like a river than a road, with extreme cold damp conditions, when we have had to have de-humidifiers running twenty four hours and producing ten litres of water each per day.

Houses suffer from damp mould on the walls which has to be removed with warm water and household bleach. The gale force wind can be frightening. We had large roof tiles blown off the roof and they landed some fifty meters away. A tree in our garden with a four inch trunk snapped like a match stick after a wind storm.

Some friends of ours had a thunderbolt of lightning smash through their window, hit all four walls and fried all of the electricity system, narrowly missing his partner before fizzing out on the floor.

Whilst writing this chapter we had an earthquake which shook the house, did some damage to a window lintel, made part of a dry stone wall collapse and measured four point five on the Richter scale. So people should not expect to be basking in the sun and heat during the winter months, although to be fair we do get some lovely warm weeks.

These weather patterns have not changed in the past twenty seven years. To give an example of how much rain we have had over the years, we have a systerna measuring 3 x 3 x 3 metres and needs two to three tanker loads of water a week to fill it in the summer months. We have now fitted gutters to the house in order to fill the systerna in winter and from November to April we do not normally have to buy any tanker water, as it is filled by the rain. Having said all this, during the winter we still experience wonderful sunny days where we can sunbathe, albeit with a very cold back!

Although Evora is not in the Algarve but in the Alentejo, in 2006 an unusual phenomenon took place when the whole city was covered in snow, this had never been known in living memory.

So having got all the negative weather off our chests, let's examine the positive aspects. The summer weather in the Algarve is and always has been absolute bliss, with over three thousand hours of glorious golden sunshine, better than the Spanish Costa Brava, Mallorca or the French Riviera and also compares very well with lots of other warm countries in the world.

The temperature of the Atlantic sea tends to be a bit cooler that the Mediterranean, the temperature of the water has not changed, is still around 22/23 degree's for most of the summer and could be a shade more in August/September. The west coast tends to be a few degrees cooler than the south, which is favoured more with holidaymakers. The general ambient temperatures also have not changed and the area has the best of both worlds, being mostly pleasantly mild in the winter and not too hot in the summer, although August can be a bit sweaty. None of this has changed even due to the so called nonsense called Global Warming.

It is interesting to note that from our observations of the weather patterns, the Moon has much more effect on the changes in weather than we would have expected. It seems that in the summer months when we see a new or old Moon, the weather can often change; so if it is very calm and hot, the Moon can change the climate to windy, cool and vice-versa. As a non-scientific study we have noticed that in the Spring and Autumn, when it is fine and sunny in the UK, the weather here is usually wet and horrible and the opposite is true, when the UK is wet and miserable, it is glorious here.

However, in spite of everything we have found the most acceptable climate to be the spring, where pleasant warm breezes waft the heady scents of the orange blossom and please the senses. The temperatures remain as always, a comfortable heat during the day, (around 25degrees C) not too cold in the evenings and night time. Generally, it is a wonderful country with a fantastic climate and superb to visit all the year round and we love it here!

The Tavira 'Inferno' in winter weather.

CHAPTER TEN

European Union

The EU has been extremely good news for Portugal generally and the Algarve in particular. When we first came to Portugal it was classed as a third world country and many of the changes outlined earlier were brought about directly as a result of joining the EU.

The six founder countries of the Union were Belgium, France, Germany, Italy, Luxembourg and the Netherlands and in 1957 the Treaty of Rome created the European Economic Community (EEC) originally called the Common Market. In 1973 Denmark, Ireland and Great Britain joined, thereby raising the number of states to nine.

Prior to the UK joining, we had a national referendum to decide whether we joined or not. Prior to the vote we decided that in order understand and have an informed opinion, we should know more about the workings of the Union. We therefore went to a six week evening class course to understand what it was all about. Rightly or wrongly, we left the tutorial with the understanding that the main thrust of the Union was to secure lasting peace in Europe, (which was one of Churchill's objectives) to scrap trade barriers, ensure the free movement of goods, where people could live, and work, also remove restrictive practices which interfered with these matters. Of course, in reality the Treaty of Rome outlined much more than this but was not commonly known.

In 1986 Portugal and Spain joined and the economy of Portugal and its people really started to improve. There were joint agreements to control excessive food production so that everyone had enough to eat and there was even overproduction of agricultural products. We have all heard of the wine lakes and food mountains, which we had, when people in other countries in the world were starving.

In 1987 the Single European Act was signed and created the 'Single Market' which was completed with the 'Four Freedoms' of: Movement of goods, Services, People and Money: border controls were relaxed and in some cases scrapped. Before the treaty, at one time we were only allowed to take £250.00 out of the UK. Of course now we can take out any amount, although we understand that anything over £1000.00 in cash must be declared.

With the start of EU regional policy, Portugal began to receive huge sums of money in order to create jobs and improve the infrastructure, which has been wonderful for the country. The Algarve has benefited enormously from EU aid and this has also helped the tourist industry to flourish. But there is no such thing as a 'free lunch' and at some point Portugal knew they would have to start paying their way and start contributing their share of finance to support other new EU Countries.

As a result of Portugal's political past, they seem very reluctant to give up some of their existing practices and fall in line with the rest of Europe. These challenges are starting to damage the Algarve's ability to attract and retain other nationalities wishing to settle or run businesses in the area, which in turn creates jobs and would improve the tourist industry. Just some of the few of many examples are listed below:-

Non-residents must pay a Fiscal Representative to pay their fiscal fees, e.g. rates, car tax and other expenses due to the Council.

Other EU members cannot keep a vehicle in the country for more than six months without matriculating it (registering under a new Portuguese number plate) into Portugal. Our last enquiry about this for our English car was the cost would be around €10,000.00. In the UK it would be under £50.00! What happens if we then want to return to the UK after six months and two weeks?

Car drivers must carry all their documents in original form, no copies allowed. In the winter damp this is very difficult. Foreign drivers are also not allowed under any circumstances to drive a Portuguese registered private car.

Excessive taxes are imposed on some goods which are not set in other EU countries. According to our Port Wine maker friend there are still restrictive practices regarding the payment of VAT at border controls.

All of these matters are in contradiction with the EU policy of the 'four freedoms' and are harming the Algarve in its current recession.

Hopefully these challenges will be overcome by the Government and the country will be more prosperous as a result. We have great hopes and are enthusiastic that our chosen hosts will become prosperous again.

CHAPTER ELEVEN

New Activities

Perhaps we were not spending enough time in the area in the early days to get immersed in local activities but as our memory serves us, we cannot remember too much going on outside of the traditional Portuguese social scene.

Looking back over the last ten/fifteen years it seems to us that there are an enormous amount of new ventures and leisure activities to do which are now occupying holiday makers and locals alike and we mention but a few.

On the beach it is now a far cry from lying basking in the Sun and doing not much else. We can now Para-glide over the sea, towed from a powerful motor speed boat, not only on our own but together with a friend on the same parachute and returning safely back to the beach under instruction from the ride attendant, as he guides us onto the sand with hand signals when we come into land. For those who would like even more excitement, we can take a hectic ride on the sea, (towed again by a fast speedboat) on an enormous yellow floating banana, seating up to eight courageous riders all of whom know that at the end of the ride they will be ditched unceremoniously into the briny, after the boat executes a fast reverse turn.

Much to the annoyance to some who prefer the quiet life on the beach, one can hire a Jet Ski and race around at very high speed with much high pitch noise. Unfortunately one swimmer was killed when being struck by such a machine. Boat trips can be chartered carrying only a few people, to some with many more on cruises, enjoying overnight stays on board; some ocean going, others on day trips or just a quick jaunt around the headland to see local caves.

Open sea scuba diving can now be undertaken for those who wish to plumb the depths of the ocean and novices can be trained using well tested training systems such as PADI, which gets people safely proficient in a very short space of time.

There are now many garden clubs up and down the Algarve and some are very hard to enter into and individuals have to be proposed by an existing member, only after a new vacancy has occurred. They have been formed by the Dutch, German and English communities and there is also a Mediterranean Society which is Pan European. The Sao Bras Museum also has its own club. There are often prizes for individual plants, flowers and whole gardens. The members meet on a regular basis, often with talks from experts who can give accurate answers to difficulties members have in growing plants and trees in the Algarve's harsh climate. Much of the music played on our arrival was very traditional Portuguese in style and, as mentioned earlier, still exists today but over the years much more modern pop and jazz music is in evidence, some of which is played so loudly it could burst the eardrums! There is now live music played almost everywhere in bars and restaurants with some musicians playing for free. Regularly, about once a month in the winter, the Sao Bras Museum stages classical music, ranging from Opera Singing to Chamber Music, Piano and Classical Guitar recitals and Jazz, all of which are all very well attended by different nationalities and entry is very reasonably priced. There is also the Algarve Orchestra, which performs outside concerts funded partly, we think by the EU.

A new innovation is the emergence of the English Pub Quiz night where all contestants are expected to set new questions for the team to answer. Again most of the quizzers are foreign nationals and sessions are often held in individuals own houses.

There are numerous book clubs, normally limited to six participants and each month a book is selected. The members have to read the contents and at end of the next month, discuss their views and opinions on the book.

Horse riding for the disabled has been organised and has been a great success. Our friend Sally, who we mentioned in ex-pats, has been a tower of strength in this operation. Our only involvement is to save all the corks from our wine bottles and these are used to cover the riding areas to protect the riders should they fall. We think that with the amount of wine we drink, they are never short of a soft landing!

Charities now abound all over the Algarve mostly staffed by non-Portuguese, as we are told that generally speaking, they do not agree with charity and that most things should be supplied by the State. The charities normally fall into four categories: Dogs, cats and donkeys. The elderly, poor and infirm, The Bombeiros (the fire brigade which is staffed mostly by volunteers) Children and orphans.

The Church of England is now very firmly established in the area and in the early days the Roman Catholic Church in Santa Barbara was used for Sunday worship. Most of the congregation, as in the UK, are elderly and when asking the local Vicar why this was so, he said that the answer was simple, 'they are all cramming for their finals'!

In Gorjoe's an English lady, Mary Reid, who runs elderly accommodation in the UK, has built a sheltered accommodation village called Palageira in Gorjoe's, where older people can buy modest one two or three bedroomed houses, some with swimming pools, surrounded by beautiful landscaped gardens. There is a three hole golf practice area and a communal pool. The complex is also linked to a small nursing home with a resident nurse and visiting English doctor which they can use. In addition to her acumen in building the Village, she has also built a modern circular Anglican Church on the site called St Luke's, which can seat some one hundred fifty worshipers and has now taken the place of the Roman Catholic Church in Santa Barbara.

We cannot leave this chapter on new activities without mentioning a really unique situation that has happened in the last year; that is the formation of the Algarve Senior Bikers. Never before has a situation like this occurred in the Algarve. A gentleman called David Shirley in his early 70s, a motorcyclist who has been involved with motorbikes all his life, moved to the area some four years ago and enjoyed riding around the Algarve on his own, which seemed a bit lonely. So to relieve the loneliness he placed an advert in the local newspapers and had a presentation on Kiss FM by Sir Owen G Window, asking anyone who wished to ride with him to meet in the Porches Bar, on June 12th 2010, where he will be waiting between 11.00am and 3.00pm. To his surprise twenty five bikers arrived to join in the ride, which was a great success.

He then took photographs of the assembled few and posted them in the same newspaper, advertising the group as the 'Algarve Senior Bikers', mature gentlemen bikers who enjoyed the company of other like individuals and may like to join the group. The response amazed him and everyone who has heard of the venture. The group mushroomed within a year to a staggering eighty five members with a web site which receives 2000 hits per month!

The group meets monthly and rides around some of the most beautiful parts of the Algarve, stopping at cafés and a break for lunch where the members swap motorcycles yarns and informing all of the latest news (not necessarily related to bikes): as one new member said 'I have learned more about the area over lunch than I have heard in three years'!

At one venue around thirty bikers appeared at a small square near Monchique to stop for coffee and as they all roared up dressed in black leather, you could see the locals thinking it was a group of Hells Angels who were going to smash the place up: but after taking off the crash helmets and showing white hair and balding heads, then sitting quietly drinking coffee, they relaxed.

The members are a very diverse group of people of both sexes aged between fifty five and mid-eighties, mostly retired (but not all) ranging from a Knight of the Realm to a boat captain and a mature lady biker who sports a Harley Davidson 1800 cc Road King! A truly international group of people including Portuguese, Dutch, English, Swedish, Welsh and Scouse! The bikes are as different as the people, ranging from maxi scooters at 650cc to large beasts that people of a certain age should not be riding!

The member's careers are as different as their bike's, some have been CEO's of large multi-national companies working all over the world, others with backgrounds in the entertainment business, artisans from the building trade, engineers, oil rig workers and engineers and a Health and Safety Officer, all with a common interests and passion for these two wheeled monsters.

The bikers now have the opportunity of wearing black ASB tee shirts and black baseball caps complete with the ASB motif. They even have their own mascot, Harley the Dog!

One year later ASB had a five minute spot on the radio station KISS FM to celebrate its first anniversary, which will no doubt swell membership numbers. Such is the advertising and exposure of the group, restaurants are now calling David to see if he would want to bring the group to their establishments. Of course with the income from thirty to forty customers for one lunch, we can see why.

This June 2011, sees the celebration of the first anniversary party of the group at the bar where it all started.

Anyone interested in joining, contact 'Algarve Senior Bikers' web site, at WWW. Algarve Senior Bikers.Org

CHAPTER TWELVE

After twenty seven years, some things have not changed.

M ost of this chapter relates to the country areas around where we live but will probably apply to most country villages in the Algarve and Portugal in general. The Portuguese country people have rarely changed their ways in twenty seven years. We call them 'country people' rather than the French word 'peasant' as this does have a rather demeaning context in our modern English language.

WATER AND SEWERAGE

Tony, our water man.

Tony our water delivery man has just called on Christmas Eve 2010 and delivered Christmas presents to us, a very traditional Portuguese Christmas cake and bottle of very nice Port. A lovely man who also runs one of the local bars and has delivered our water in a tanker ever since we first had a house here. As mentioned earlier, from the first day we came to the Algarve we never had mains water or sewerage. The water is delivered in a tanker (at great cost) and takes three loads a week in the summer, to fill our systerna. Our waste water and sewerage flows into a cess pit called a Fossa and this has never been emptied in our time here and works perfectly. Although once we joined the EU many years ago, it was deemed that all properties should have fresh mains water; we are still waiting! Hot off the press!! We have just heard that the local Camara (Council) has started the work on mains water and sewerage and the rumour is it will be finished in two years' time. If you believe that you will believe anything!

To demonstrate some Portuguese humour; when we were renewing our car insurance, we mentioned to the agent that we were going to get mains water and she said, not in our lifetime! We said no, you are wrong because they are laying the pipes in the road as we speak. To which she replied. Yeah, but that does not mean to say they will fill them with water! Watch this space!!!

FISH

The fish man still delivers vast quantities of fresh cheap fish daily in a small white van, with very loud alpine horns which wake us all up around eight-o-clock most days. It stops at the same predetermined places on the road, weighs out and sells the fish to the locals, mostly sardines, which has been their staple diet for years.

GIPSIES

The Gipsies still travel around in their gaily painted horse and carts, with many small children in and hanging all over the sides of the cart, usually laughing and playing around. The cart normally has another animal or two in tow to the rear, perhaps an Ass or a Donkey as a spare! The family dogs trot under the cart in its shadow to keep out of the hot sun. They still build makeshift camps out of any material that will make a shelter, usually old scraps of canvass, polythene and tarpaulin held together with string poles and ropes. Their clothes and washing is thrown over bushes and trees to dry in the sun. The Gipsy women still wear traditional black or coloured dresses down to the ankles. When we researched why this was so, it appears that in the Gipsy culture, anything below the female waist was deemed to be unclean and must be covered! How much of this has been determined by the men, we leave to conjecture. When Gipsy children are born, irrespective of what the child is named, the mother will whisper in the child's ear a secret name, in addition to the given name, only the child and mother will ever know the secret.

BREAD

We still see plastic bags hung from trees, with money left inside, waiting for the bread van to come. A note inside the bag indicating what type of bread and how much is required, which the bread man will leave until collected. We never heard of any money being stolen from the bags. This practice is fast disappearing, as more people use their cars to travel to supermarkets

CAROBS, OLIVES AND ALMONDS

Locals in August, normally very early in the cool of the morning around six am, continue to harvest the Alfarobas (Carobs) by using a long springy pole which they rattle amongst the branches of the tree until the Carobs drop to the ground, they are then put into large hessian sacks to be sold. It is not unusual to see one harvest of twenty or thirty sacks per person. Depending on the yield of the year, a sack can fetch a significant amount of money.

Whilst on the subject of Carob sticks, we had a hilarious situation occurred with such a stick. In the picking season it is quite normal to see local country people with a stick tied to the roof of their car, with the end protruding out at the front. We thought in order to be seen as 'local' we would buy a stick and tie it to the top of our Mehari. So one red hot day in August, returning from the beach in the Mehari, we were wearing not much more than a smile, Fay shouted out, stop the car! stop the car! I thought she might have had a heart attack or some such tragedy but no, she had seen some Carob sticks for sale in a very small, old traditional hardware shop, in a tiny quiet country road. She ordered me to go and buy a stick. Not likely I said, I am virtually naked. Fay was looking like a Dior model and drop dead gorgeous, with an extremely skimpy red bikini, which only just covered her modesty. Without any further ado, she leapt from the car, ran across the road, barefoot and proceeded to buy the stick from a very old wrinkled country gentleman, who had probably not seen such a body since his younger days. Well; his eyes were as big as saucers and his jaw dropped almost down to the floor and we expect to this day he has never seen anything like it, and is still talking about it and trying to pick his jaw up from the ground!

Olives are harvested by laying large sheet of cloth under the tree and shaking the trunk and branches until the fruit drops onto the sheets. Quite often we can see whole families getting involved in the task. Only last week we saw a family of Gipsies in the middle of a road roundabout, picking the Olives. Again these are put into sacks and sold to the local Olive Press or exchanged for litres of Olive Oil. The amount paid is dependent of the weight of Olives collected.

The rosy pink glow of the flowers of the leafless almond trees, continue to delight the eye and lift the spirit as they blossom in January and February. The hillsides covered in their snow like appearance of the blossom keep the legend of the Nordic Princess alive.

SHEPHERDS

The Shepherds and Goatherds still tend their animals in the fields. They can be seen sitting on a rock wall clutching a bottle of water or beer, with their lunch, with a David and Goliath sling shot or catapult in their belt, ready to ward off anything that may endanger their flocks. Their dogs are always at the ready to stop the animals straying into the roads or other dangerous places. The men look as old as Methuselah but because of the harsh hot climate, are probably only twenty five years old!!

DOGS

The millions of dogs owned by the locals continue to boredom bark when anything causes them to, like a worm crossing the road!! The Portuguese will say they are a nation of dog lovers but they are not. They are a nation of dog keepers and chain the wretched animals up night and day and the barking drives us round the bend!!! If there was one reason why we would leave the Algarve, it would be the incessant barking. The only time they do not bark is when it rains. Sometimes they bark all around the valley and get into a barking frenzy, just like sharks in a feeding frenzy.

When we first arrived, there were packs of wild dogs roaming the streets, beaches and countryside and they were quite frightening to be near, what with rabies and all. At the crossroads in Gorjoe's there used to be so many packs of dogs it was locally known as 'dog corner' One year we bought some new lounger pads for the seats around the pool and the very next night the dogs came into the pool area and ripped them to pieces so badly we had to throw them away.

When we were travelling a local road we saw a dead dog thrown into the ditch, probably hit by a vehicle. It was laying on its back with its feet up in the air and stiff as a board. Some weeks later we were travelling down the same road and the carcass was still in the same place but someone had poured petrol over it and set it alight, the stench was putrid and flies were crawling and buzzing all over the carcass. To this day we still call the road 'dead dog road!

Now we have official dog catchers with vans, they round up any dog that does not have a collar and as far as we know they are put to sleep.

Nothing changes with these canine pests, they continue as they have always done throughout time immemorial, when the full moon is high in the midnight sky, they howl and whine at it until daybreak. Nice!

OLD MEN.

On most corners and road T-junctions, we see old men sitting or standing watching the world go by and putting the world to rights, as they have done for ever and a day. They stop talking as we walk or ride by and stare until we are gone. Most times they have the traditional bottle of beer in their hands, irrespective of the time of day and become more vocal as the day goes by.

POP, POP MOTORBIKES

When we arrived here, old country men and women would ride the cheapest form of transport which was the clapped out pop-pop motorbikes. They are powered by small two stroke engines with the silencers removed from the exhaust pipes, so very noisy; with much damage to our eardrums. Twenty five years later, the same bikes can be seen, rusty and falling to bits but still in use. Often they are loaded with bags of shopping, bales of hay and other country articles all hanging over the sides.

CEREAL CROPS

We still see crops harvested by hand, men and women bent double, reaping crops with scythes and cycles, tying them into string tied sheaves, then dotting them around the fields to dry in the burning sun.

WATER WELLS AND WATER CARTS.

As mentioned earlier, most water is delivered by a water tanker, that is for those of us that can afford the very high prices. Poorer folk still draw water from the local wells with a bucket and rope, then in turn, empty the water into one or two twenty five litre galvanised urns, to be hauled in a custom made hand cart back to their homes. Most of these folk are bent over the cart pushing them up and down hills and far too old to be drawing water in this fashion. Until recently all the wells had open tops and we often wondered if any children had been drowned by falling into them but we never heard of any. They now all have metal grills fixed over the top secured by a padlock.

COMMUNAL WASHING HOUSES.

There are still white washed concrete wash houses by the side of the road and the local women, (in addition to all the other mundane tasks they have to perform) can be seen chatting away, with bars of soap, hand washing their clothes and bashing them clean on flat ribbed stone areas.

EASTER PIGS

One of our local country families keeps pigs, with the resulting noise and odour! Every Easter we hear the shrieks of the pig as it is slaughtered for the Easter feast. Not a sound that we are used to in the UK.

WIDOWS BLACK AND HATS

When a husband dies, it is traditional for the wife to go into black clothes for the rest of her life and this still happens in our area. Even some quite young widows continue with the custom. One alternative was, that the widow would dress in traditional country clothing but in addition, will wear the dead husbands Sunday best Trilby hat, held down with a scarf tied under the chin.

STARING

One of the most disconcerting habits of the local's, is their need to stare at everything and anybody within their gaze. This might be somebody walking past or making a comment to them or passing in a car. They stare almost until we are out of sight. It is not seen as rude, as it would be in the UK but part of their normal behaviour. We were told when we first moved here, that if they were really upset about something we had done, they would stare at our feet. However we have never seen it happen nor had it done to us.

FOLK DANCING (FADO)

Although in the past there has been an enormous increase in the Pop culture with extremely loud pop group music in evidence but the country folk still stick to the traditional folk music and dance called Fado. It can be regularly heard on the radio and local Danceteiras in the summer where they hold folk dance evenings.

At the millennium of 2000 the people of Gorjoe's decided to have a village celebration to mark the event; (the organisation is called Clube Recreativo E Cultural Gorjonese) so they built a stage in the village and invited a famous Fado group to perform, which was a roaring success. They enjoyed the dance and feasting so much, they now hold dances most weeks in the summer months and people come from miles around to join in the festivities. Some come in cars and many in coachloads. Many locals still dress in traditional country dress, carrying farm implements used long ago. Scythes, shovels, pitchforks, water vessels and olive jars perched on the shoulder, and various other ancient farming tools are displayed, as they process from the centre of the village or hamlet to the dancing areas. This is not confined to the older folk.

We saw two boy babies born in the house next to our housekeeper's when we first moved here, they are now in their twenties, have learned with great flare, the old dance movements and perform them with great gusto at the dances, sometimes complete with fag hanging from the mouth.

We have been to many of these events and they are most enjoyable. Whole families complete with mums, dads, kids and grandparents attend and they all mix very sociably with each other with no apparent age divide.

On one very rare occaision a man who we had never seen in the village, so we guessed he was an outsider; very portly with large protruding stomach and very, very drunk, (our third instance of drunkenness) insisted on dancing with a young married lady and proceed to grope her in a most unseemly manner. Obviously her husband tried to part the couple and the drunk then hit husband and a fight broke out with all the young fit boys joining in. They were picking up plastic chairs, hitting people over the heads with them and a general mêlée took place for a few minutes. The locals all stood up and a look of utter disgust was on all their faces. There had never been anything like it before or since. However the GNR were on duty and within no time at all, they very unceremoniously escorted the drunk out of the dance. To our knowledge he has never attended another dance, nor has there been any more trouble of this kind.

OLD PEOPLE SITTING OUTSIDE DOORS

In the hot summer months it is still usual to see older people sitting outside the front door of their Casa, taking in the fresh air and the view, sheltering in the shade. Even when the house is on the side of a busy road, they sit amongst the noise and dust of the traffic. In the winter which we have said can be very cold and damp, people still do not heat their houses but put on more and more clothes. It is very normal to see the country folk walking around the roads wearing layers of all their normal day clothes and in addition they will wear a dressing gown over the top with furry goatskin slippers on their feet.

THE GREENHOUSE EFFECT AND GLOBAL WARMING

In 1978 we were told by the worlds 'experts' that due to the way we are all abusing our planet and our excessive use of fossil fuels (naughty us) we will experience the polar ice caps melting with the sea levels rising to excessive limits (one English politician stated by sixteen feet!) and many islands would disappear. Faro airport is built very close to the Atlantic coast and only a few feet above sea level, yet thirty three years later after the prophets of doom pontificated on the Global Warming scam, the sea levels around the mudflats on the airport landing approach, are still the same. Also the many low level salt pans still deposit their crusty white salt, derived from the sea as they have done for centuries since Phoenician times.

DUSTBINS

Large Grundon type dustbins are the only way of disposing of household rubbish and this system has not changed. In the summer the stink of rotting rubbish is something to behold. In our village we used to have single bins dotted around, close enough for people to walk with their rubbish. This has not changed except where there were single bins there are now as many as six or seven. The stray (and no so stray) dogs, cats and rats, still strew the contents all over the place, seeking scraps of food and the resulting rubbish is blown in the adjacent fields. In larger towns they have now been replaced by underground concrete pits with stainless steel entry columns and this is much more hygienic.

ROADS

The majority of the country roads continue to be covered with pot holes with the road crumbling into the dirt edges. If one is lucky, once every one or two years some men will arrive with a lorry full of Tarmac, throw some into the holes and wait for the traffic to flatten the Tarmac with their wheels. This lasts until it rains and then gets washed out in no time.

THE BEACHES

They have always been and still are some of the most beautiful beaches in the world. From the wide Atlantic rollers on the Silver Coast loved by the surf riders, to the craggy Rocha beaches and the wide expansive silver sandy beaches in the south; they are a great hit with young and old, holidaymakers and locals alike.

A West Coast Beach

BUREAUCRACY

Ever since the Revolution when Salazar the dictator took control of the country, the populace has been controlled with bureaucracy and excessive paperwork. In Spain, Franco controlled the people with oppressive violence. In Portugal it was bureaucracy. Now we are in the EU, very little has changed and the very patient Portuguese people, still accept the status quo and are used to waiting and queuing for the smallest bit of service from the overstaffed civil servants. Although computers have now taken over so many mundane tasks, the paperwork is still excessive, over burdening and both local government and businesses remain over staffed.

If ever there was a reason for us leaving the Algarve (apart from the dogs) the following article from the Portugal News newspaper would be the one.

'EXPATS TO FOOT THE BILL FOR PORTUGAL

DEBT

Following the resignation of Prime Minister Jos'e Socrates last week, Portugal's opposition parties have clubbed together to introduce a new tax on all EU citizens currently residing in the country or with property in Portugal.

PSD opposition party leader, Pedro Passas Lebre made the announcement public in parliament this week while Jos'e Socrates and the President were engaged in talks with His Royal Highness the Prince of Wales.

'Our people cannot take any more of the PS government's austerity measures. We cannot squeeze any more money out of them but we can squeeze more money out of the foreign community that have come to live in our country' he said.

Due to a loophole in Portuguese law, the joining of all the country's opposition parties to vote on the secret measure in parliament after the Prime Minister resigned, means that this law has been provisionally passed until a new Prime Minister is elected.

For expats, it will mean increased taxes on all goods in supermarkets, DIY stores and fuel stations as they will have to produce identification at the tills in all shops. Water, electricity and gas bills will also see rises in the tax to the government for all foreigners.

The tax legislation will also have specific tax rates for different nationalities of citizens living in Portugal, with those from former Portuguese colonies such as Brazil, Angola and Mozambique, as well as citizens from Eastern European countries not being affected by these tax hikes.

Dutch, German and Scandinavian citizens will be charged 25% more taxes in Portugal, while the British have been hit with the biggest tax hike at 50%.

'We have decided to penalise the British because there are so many of them and their country decided not to join the single currency' said one MP. This new last minute legislation was due to come into effect on April 1st. (April Fool!)

By kind permission of Paul Luckman. The Portugal News.

GNR (THE POLICE)

The GNR (Guardia National Republica) continue (and always have done in our twenty five year experience) to pursue and harass all drivers of any vehicle, with random roadside blocks, checking for the correct authority papers. They check driving licences, insurance certificates, identity cards, passports, test certificates and this happens whether one is a tourist or resident. All papers must be the originals and copies are not acceptable. The checks take around half an hour and wobetide anyone who is not absolutely correct with the papers. The fines for non-compliance are horrendous. We understand that the police work on commission and we can tell by their body language that they are visibly disappointed if all is correct. In a commercial vehicle it is mandatory to carry a paper stapler! Don't ask!!

A friend of ours runs a small business doing odd jobs for English residents, has been stopped in his van twenty two times in the past three years. On the last occasion he had two light bulbs in their original packaging, for which he could not produce the original sales invoice. His licence was confiscated by the police and his wife had to spend a total of eight hours the next day at the local Finances filling out papers, answering stupid questions and was fined €20.00!! When she asked for his driving licence back, they said she was not authorised to take it and had to go back the next day with a letter of authority from her husband, written in Portuguese, together with the original copy of her marriage certificate. This is in 2010 in the EU. It really does defy comment!

KNIVES AND CHESTNUTS

The shrill sound of plastic Pan Pipes of the knife sharpening man can be heard in the Algarve. He rides around the streets and villages on a bicycle seeking knives to sharpen. His bike is old and rickety and he has a large triangular support which raises the back wheel off the ground. The rear wheel has a massive pulley with a leather belt spinning a smaller pulley, which has a small grinding wheel fitted to the crossbar. He sits on the bike pedalling the back wheel to make the grinding wheel spin and with this contraption he sharpens the knives. He is not seen so much these days, as with the advent of inexpensive imported knives, it is cheaper to buy a new knife that have the old ones sharpened.

The old tradition of roasting chestnuts still can be seen in towns and villages around Christmas time. The chestnut man has a roasting fire on a three wheeled support similar to an ice cream sellers bicycle and he sells the piping hot nuts wrapped up in old sheets of Yellow Pages paper.

TRAVEL TO SUPERMARKETS.

As mentioned earlier it is still common to see the country folk using very modern supermarkets and travelling to them in a farm lorry or a tractor, sometimes with the woman sitting in a large bucket attachment at the rear of the vehicle.

MOTHBALLED SCHOOLS

Most villages have a small school for the local children and the education system seems very effective. When the children grow up and have to go to senior schools or there are no children left the village to fill the school, the building is 'mothballed'. It will be opened again when future generations of children are born. It is also used as a communal meeting place for social events. It seems a very sensible and inexpensive way of using the building.

GRACIOSA

When we bought our first house here, our builder introduced us to Graciosa, a lady who lived at the bottom of our track and she was to become our 'Maid'. This word again we do not like, as it does smack of servility, so we have always called her our housekeeper. She is a highly intelligent 'rotund' lady with a ready smile, laughing face and a great sense of humour. She takes very seriously the responsibility of looking after our home when we are not there. She has been our support and rock in the Algarve for twenty six years. She looks after the house, cleans like a white tornado, terrifies the tradesmen and after all this time she is just as efficient, conscientious and caring as she was the first day we met.

Now in her sixties she and her husband José look after ours and a number of other houses on our hill. Sometimes we think, that they think, we are still the crazy English kids that they met all those years ago, and still treat us as such, even though we are probably older than they are! On many occasions when we arrive in the winter, the log fire is lit, crackling and sizzling away, there are always fresh flowers around the house and the electric blanket in the bed is turned on. What a treasure!

THE QUIET DIGNIFIED FRIENDLY PORTUGUESE PEOPLE.

One thing that seems perennial, is the lovely nature of our country Portuguese people. They have a quiet, conservative dignity about them and an extremely friendly disposition to us, the English, Estrangeiros (strangers). Even though we bring to them some strange customs, seemingly unheard of wealth and a way of living, so different to their ways; they still carry on with their way of life as they have done for centuries, as we do ours, with no outward effect on either of us. A couple of interesting aspects of the people is, they do not fully understand the English humour of sarcasm. They revel and laugh at anything where individuals suffer hardship, like falling over or out of a tree etc. As an example, a man falls of a ladder and breaks his leg, ha ha, ha! Another joke told by the Portuguese against themselves. A young pubescent lad who has just started growing some hair on his top lip is asked by a man 'Are you growing a moustache like your dad, no he replies, just like my mum!'

However, they have profited very well from the sale of their land and properties on which we build our houses, the additional employment they have gained from building work and maid cleaning services have been a boon to them.

We sold our original house and now have now built another, a hundred metres up the hill, with two acres of garden which we fully maintain ourselves. We continue to grow old disgracefully, roaring around the Algarve on our big hairy Intruder, 1800cc blue and cream motorcycle, covered in chrome, leather and studs, (which we fell off twice last week in the same day) when most folks of our age are in slippers, sitting in front of the fire, and watching the soaps on television. Next year off to Tibet touring on a Yak!

The sun continues to set every evening, and spreads its fiery cloak of red, crimson, and pink tinged clouds over the green panoramic landscape covered with almond, fig, pomegranate and palm trees; and the crickets softly sing their scratchy song as they have done forever. Over the years we have experienced the most magnificent sunsets we have seen anywhere in the world. Now we watch again with a cool glass of Portuguese wine in our hands, munching bowls full of nuts and crisps, watching yet another superb sunset and if we listen carefully we can hear the hisssss as the orange sun disappears into the azure sea.

CHAPTER THIRTEEN

Miscellaneous

We have included this chapter because some of the interesting matters not covered elsewhere deserve comment, and do not fit comfortably in other parts of the book, but none the less are part of our Algarve history and are well worth a mention.

In Loul'e there used to be a character the locals called the 'Man/Lady. 'It' was about five feet six tall, portly and was dressed in women's finery of fishnet stockings and a Mini Skirt, high heeled shoes, very smart frilly blouse covered with a fitted jacket. The face was made up to the nines with thick lipstick, powder and makeup, long black hair and a beret. The face sporting an enormous black moustache!

He/she would walk around the busy parts of the town laughing out loud to itself and singing at full pitch, the most wonderful opera aria's in two very splendid distinct male and female voices. The female being extremely high pitched and the other male and very deep baritone. The pitch of the voice was always perfect, in tune with the song and the male/female parts could change mid-sentence! It has not been seen around for many years and one often wonders what became of he/she.

Another character in our village of Gorjoe's was 'Miguel' he was as much use as last year's turnips and could be quite frightening to those not familiar with his strange ways. He was what most people would call a tramp but not the 'gentleman of the road' one would expect to see in the UK. Dressed in brown rags from top to toe he stayed mainly around the village. His clothes were so shabby and torn with holes all over the place, the seat of his pants were mostly missing and as he ran down the road with a shambling gait, from the back we could see his testicles swinging two and fro. Not a pretty sight and one to be avoided!

He spent most of his life roaming the fields piling up rocks and stones for what reason only he knew. He also carried an axe of which we were very nervous. He would appear all of a sudden on the boundary of our land and start chopping down branches and trees of which we were trying to cultivate. When we shouted to him to stop he would roll his eyes in a most disconcerting fashion, laugh like a maniac and continue with his task. We certainly would not get too close to him or his axe! We lost many a good tree at his hands. Local rumour said he was an ex Portuguese soldier who had been damaged in battle but we were not sure about this. In any event he was one sandwich short of a pic-nick. All of a sudden he was not seen any more, presumably dead but we all slept more comfortably afterwards. There is a chap in Faro operating a scam through which presumably makes a living. He is extremely well dressed, normally in a suit, collar and tie.

His is Portuguese and speaks with a very upper class cut glass English accent and could be taken for a member of the aristocracy. He starts his patter by asking if we are English and then goes into his spiel. I have lost my wallet and need urgently to get to Lisbon by train, could we possibly help him with the fare. He is very polite, plausible and we have seen many a tourist fall for his guile and give him money. We first met him twenty five years ago but did not give him anything. Then blow me down we saw him last week when he approached us with exactly the same story. When we told him that he tried the same trick on us some twenty years ago he just laughed and said that a Euro would do and when we refused he just walked up to another stranger and tried again!

Travel anywhere in the world through country parts it is soon obvious when we reach so called 'civilisation' On the outskirts of towns and cities, the areas are blighted by Graffiti and this is also the same in the Algarve. In Venice as an example, which is reputedly one of the most beautiful cities in the world with magnificent buildings and canals, the whole place is covered with graffiti. The Rialto Bridge, probably the most photographed monument, is also riddled with this foul trash. In tourist brochures the Graffiti is air brushed out, so it is a bit of a shock when first seen by newcomers. When arriving by air at Faro airport and driving through the exit road, the graffiti starts and continues all along the EN125 and into the towns.

Of course there has been some form of graffiti as long as there has been civilisation. In early times, one drawing depicted Jesus crucified with the head of a donkey, suggesting that only a fool would be put in a position to be crucified.

In 1984 there was a small amount of 'tagging' around but it has increased year by year and really devalues the tourist attractions in this beautiful part of the world. It seems that neither the police nor the authorities are interested in cleaning it up or catching and punishing the offenders. Yet the solution is cheap, easy and simple to implement, as shown by one alleyway in Loul'e, which for years has been the delight of the graffiti vandals. The whole of the tunnel's graffitied walls were painted over with white paint and as soon as the walls were defaced, so they were painted over again. The problem has disappeared and the alley is always clear.

The sadness is that graffiti is classed as criminal damage and as such is legally a punishable offence. This and the drugs menace has been dubbed as the gateway to crime, yet both do not seem to be important by the authorities. Yet if we as motorist break a minor traffic offence we are castigated and fined immediately. An easy target?

One night we had been asleep for about four hours, when we were woken with such a start with an explosion so great, that we thought an aircraft had crashed not one kilometre away. Either that or we thought it was an enormous earthquake. The building and the ground shook to the point where we were considering vacating the house. It was very frightening. We rushed to the window to see flames leaping into the night sky and then there was another great explosion followed by what seemed to be an enormous free firework display. This continued for the next half an hour, even Disney could not have put up such a show. Eventually the reality of the situation dawned upon us. It was not a plane crash or an earthquake. Not far from us in a small village, there was a little firework factory which was in effect a ramshackle collection of wooden huts. These had caught alight, all the contents had exploded and burnt the place to the ground. The following day we went to see the damage and the factory could not be seen, other than some wooden walls lying on the ground. The police and the fire brigade were there damping down the remains and stopping nosy parkers like us from gawping at the damage, which was considerable. Nearby houses had walls knocked down and large gaping splits had appeared in some homes. Lots of very shocked neighbours were standing around in groups talking and some weeping as they looked at the damage to their property. We heard later that this had happened on two previous occasions and the rumour was that the 'accidents' were staged to collect the insurance money. However, true or not the factory was never allowed to be rebuilt.

On the subject of rebuilding, as the years went by we wanted to make improvements to the house and we had two choices in this respect. We could employ a local builder, plumber, electrician, or carpenter etc. or we could attempt the work ourselves. So having the reputation of being a couple of old skinflints and tight as a ducks bum, we decided to undertake the projects ourselves. Having been great DIY enthusiasts in the past, mainly because we have always been broke and our cash flow looks more like a cash dribble, we set about the tasks with some trepidation. The first project required the purchase of some timber, so we looked around for a store something like B&Q in the

UK. How naive! The nearest thing to a British type store was Stumpys wood yard on the road from Santa Barbara to Almancil. So we turned up expecting to see a vast array of beautifully prepared timber, in neat stacks from which we could select the wood we needed. Aha! New comers abroad were we. After negotiating our way around two or three starving Rottweiler's and a couple of mean looking Alsatian dogs, snapping snarling and barking their heads off, all of which looked determined to have us for their lunch, we found Stumpy under a pile of wood shavings and sawdust. A short round Portuguese man with a large beer belly and a ready smile, greeted us with an outstretched handshake, as all the Portuguese do when greeting friends and strangers alike. Trying to make him understand the type of timber we wanted was like talking to a Martian on another planet. However, we managed by sign language to convey the exact dimensions and type of wood we needed (we had two choices, pine or mahogany), he disappeared in his open flatbed truck and he was gone so long we thought he was having his lunch break!

After what seemed like a couple of hours, he returned on the truck with half a tree that had obviously been laying around maturing for many years. He then hoisted this great lump of timber onto an enormous band saw, which looked so old that Adam might have been using it in the Garden of Eden. He then spent the next hour sawing and planning the wood to our exact measurements. We were very impressed. The dogs were still barking and baying and looking at us with very hungry eyes. So we paid Stumpy the very small price for our purchases, carefully drove around the dogs and returned home exhausted, but well chuffed with our day.

Why do we call him Stumpy? Because over the years he had been very careless with the use of the band saw and he had cut off the ends of some fingers on one hand!

The blackbirds with their lively beautiful trilling song wake us up at dawn from our slumbers. This is such a normal event nowadays that we take it for granted but this is quite a recent phenomenon. In earlier days our hill was bereft of any birds or bird song, very similar to the silence experienced at Belson and other death camps in Germany, where birds still do not visit after the atrocities of the last World War. We found it very strange when we first moved into our new house, that there were not any birds or birdsong, as we were used to in the UK. Then on Thursdays and Sundays we realised why. The hunters and shooters were allowed to shoot anything that moved in the area where we lived. There were no boundaries to their carnage of the wildlife and they could roam at will, even into people's gardens: on one occasion we were shot at above our heads because we complained directly to the hunters. They would mostly shoot rabbits for the pot but also would bring down any raptor roaming the sky which was seeking its natural prey, rabbits and small mammals etc. It was very sad to see these beautiful birds of prey shot and lying on the ground just to satisfy the hunter's hobby.

Some years ago the situation was changed by law and designated areas were outlined, away from habitation, where the hunting was then allowed, and we understand the fines for transgressors were quite swingeing. This changed the habitat for the birds, which soon realised that the safety zones around the houses, was a good place to be and breed etc. Very soon all types of birds were to be seen, Blackbirds,

Sparrows, Doves, Eagles, Hawks, Swallows, House Martins, Bee Eaters, Hoopoe's, Storks, and Little Owls to name but a few and are now quite commonplace. It is one of the delights of life to hear the Nightingales singing away in the dead of night and to watch the Goldfinches drinking from our fountain in the cool of the afternoon. So, peace has come to the wildlife around us at last and we are all the better for being here. Sadly, now in 2011 there has new been a new law passed whereby hunters can now legally shoot up to forty Blackbirds a day, what sense does that make?

On hot summer nights between nine forty five and ten fifteen when the moon cannot be seen, we experience a wonderful sight laying on our backs on the warm terrace tiles and watching the heavens. Between these times it is quite normal to trace at least two satellites speeding across the inky black sky and usually a shooting star can be seen. This is only possible due to the fact there is very little light pollution in the Algarve, so in addition we turn all the house lights off to improve the view.

Because of these hot nights, we fitted ceiling fans to help the cooling in June, July and August and these have been a boon. But the real joy is waking in the morning, opening all the doors and windows and letting in the cool, fresh, morning air which tastes like wine!

Gardening is very much a hit and miss experience as we are virtually gardening on a mountainside. Of course there are many books on this subject, so we do not intend to dwell on the difficulties, other than to demonstrate one aspect. This is the problem of planting shrubs and trees in extremely rocky ground; the last tree we planted took three hours to dig the hole and removed over two hundredweight of rocks. The actual planting of the tree only took about ten minutes!

Whilst on the subject of plants: there is a new blight that has affected some species of Palm in the Algarve and has been devastating them over the past two years. Palms are not natural to Portugal and it is believed that originally they were imported from the Middle East and have flourished everywhere, giving the country a very attractive exotic look. However, the new imports have not been checked as thoroughly as they should have been for bugs and diseases and because of this, a nasty insect has infected the imported Palms and is killing them wholesale. Apparently the male bug burrows around in the crown of the Palm and sprays his pheromones all over the plant. The female then finds his scent and lays her eggs on top of the trunk. When the eggs hatch, the new born grubs then eat the fleshy centre of the trunk and kills the tree, causing the all the Palm fronds to droop, wither and die.

So, sadly we will eventually lose all this species of Palm and the countryside is looking the worse as a result.

In 2005 we had a most frightening experience with bush fires over the whole of Portugal and the Algarve in particular. Over our years here we have always had forest and bush fires due to the extreme dry heat in the hot summer months. However, this was the year when fires raged all over Europe, in Greece, Spain, Italy, France and Portugal with devastating results. A lot of the fires had been started deliberately, either by pyromaniacs, (sometimes it was rumoured by firemen) or builders who have tried to get permission to build on their land and had been refused on the grounds that the plot was in an area of outstanding beauty. Most of the fires are quickly put out by the local Bombeiros but one was started by some builders setting light to old cement sacks and the wind took the flames onto some dry land very close to us. At the same time bush fires were raging all over the Algarve and around us, to the point where it was dangerous to drive on the motorways due to the smoke blocking the view from the windscreen. The fire brigades just could not cope and the fires raged for some days. We had to be evacuated from our house as the fires were so close and we had hot ash falling like snow all over our property.

Eventually after a lot of lobbying of the government they chartered seven sea plane tankers from Italy and they flew in formation over our heads every seven minutes, dropping their tanks of water, then returning to land on the sea, refilling and returning to drop the next load. This continued for two or three days until all the fires were extinguished. It was like living in a war zone with the noise and heat.

Millions of hectares of land were destroyed, with the loss of thousands of trees and natural shrubs: it was a national disaster. Something had to be done to stop this happening in the future and all credit to the politicians, we now have several emergency helicopters on permanent standby ready to move as soon as smoke is detected. They load up with firemen and fire fighting equipment and rush to the fire, leaving the firemen to control the blaze before it gets out of hand. They then return to base and fill their bags with water and are back to the scene within minutes, dropping tons of water to put out the fire before it gets worse.

In addition there has been a law passed banning the lighting of bonfires during the summer months and if they are to be lit in the winter, a licence must first be obtained so the Bomberios knows where to call if it gets out of hand. The fines for transgressors are very steep. Instead of bonfires, the locals take their garden rubbish to the dustbin areas and dump it there, it does not look too good but the bin men regularly pick it up and take it to the council recycling plant, where it is turned into compost and plant food which is on sale at a very low price. So everybody wins. These measures have been successful over the years and fingers crossed; we have not had any serious fires since.

Now, we can only talk about this next subject of prostitution from folk tales and rumour, not from personal experience! In our early days here we never saw or heard any talk about prostitutes. Although it is said to be the oldest profession, rumour has it that the whole business is being ruined by amateurs!! (Joke.)

However, since the emergence of the EU and influxes of some of the more undesirable individuals from some of the Eastern European States, the area has seen a great influx of these 'ladies of the night' or in this part of the Algarve, ladies of the day as well! In 1984 we would never have seen a bare breast or midriff in a magazine or newspaper, let alone brazen prostitution. Now it appears that sex in the press and magazines is commonplace and seems to be accepted by all. In a recent survey of the free and not so free newspapers, we counted twenty eight adverts for female and male 'escorts'. They offer all sorts of services from 'classy evenings out with sophisticated girls' to blatant homosexual sex. This would never have been tolerated in earlier days but now has become commonplace. On the infamous N 125 road which runs the length of the Algarve, there is a turning which goes up to a large aggregate quarry and it seems that some of the punters could be the long distance lorry drivers hauling the gravel. On this entrance and the access road, we see many of our ladies plying their trade and this has caused complaints from locals and holidaymakers alike, especially those passing by with families. The police say there is nothing that they can do about it as the profession is not against the law.

What they charge for their services we could not know, unless we delved into the more seedy side of the profession but rumour has it that €50.00 is the going rate but we do not really wish to know. Whatever the price, it does remind us of one of the verses of a Limerick in a Rugby song;

'That was a very nice song, sing us another one just like the other one, sing us another one doooo—There was a young girl from Kilkenny, whose usual fee was a penny, for an additional sum you could tickle her tum, a source of amusement to many.

Some might know more racy words! Of course this has nothing to do with our ladies or the Algarve but might bring a smile to some folks!

Whether these girls are freelance or held in vice, we do not know but in any event we feel very sorry for them, that they need to earn a living in this way. We make no judgement or further comment other than to us it seems a sad reflection on the general lowering of standards in all sorts of areas seen throughout society these days.

One other interesting situation has happened frequently and that is the local stray cats who roam around most properties looking for food. Some of them are feral, dangerous and not to be encouraged. Others are domestic animals that probably have been abandoned and are reasonably harmless.

One such cat took a fancy to us so we fed him daily. He was on the point of death, starving, malnourished, black and white, ugly with one ear which did not have any fur, and his wedding tackle was enormous. We had some friends staying with us and they named him the Ugly Little Bastard. However, we continued to care for him. After three years he is now totally tame and domesticated, has had his wedding tackle removed and we found that his ear was cancerous so we had to have it removed. His name is Fred and he rules the household! People say that dogs have masters and cats have servants. That is certainly true where Fred is concerned!

The Portuguese people have never passed up a reason to have a rip-roaring carnival and we understand that it was them who took carnival to South America and the Latin countries. Loul'e is no exception to this rule and produce many street carnivals throughout the year, some related to religious festivals and others just for fun. One of the latest and we believe the best, is the annual White Night held at the end of the summer, where the whole of the town is decorated in everything white, buildings, shops and displays are covered in white. There are musicians, bands, fire eaters, strange white monsters roaming the town and anyone wearing white can get 20% off the products in the shops.

Two lovely girls at the White Night.

Lastly, a mention about the Portuguese language. It is an extremely difficult language to learn, even the Portuguese after learning it say that they still have problems with is vagaries. In the early days we bought a Linquaphone Portuguese language course and studied it for some long months in the UK and we were very keen to try it out when we returned to Portugal. What a disaster that was, the course was taught in the classical Lisbon style and accent, so when we tried it out on the locals they could not understand a word we said. Their accents are very local and have been quoted as being 'field Algavian' it is almost the same as a Surrey resident trying to understand a broad Glaswegian accent.

When we first arrived, very few people spoke good English, so we tried to pick up the local lingo with some very limited success. Now English is taught as a second language together with Portuguese in primary schools and it is very rare to find young people not using English. In addition, they say that they like speaking it, find it easy to learn and of course, now being in the EU which has adopted it as the common language, it is used by so many more countries. Much to the disgust of the French who wanted their language to be the common one!

We have spoken to many young people who started to learn English at school but picked up so much more by watching UK and American TV programmes, so much so that one girl sounded like Bart Simpson! When complimenting young people on their superb command of English, the normal reply is, if we do not speak English in the Algarve we cannot get a job! So we continue to struggle with the language in the shops etc. and the normal response is **'Say it in English'**!

SUMMARY

Building a second home and living part of our lives in the Algarve was the best decision we made in our married life. Meeting the lovely people of the area, trying to understand their cultures, priorities and customs has enriched our lives in a most interesting and exiting way.

Some two years later after building our first house, we walked to the top of the hill, sat on a dry stone wall and the views for miles were breath taking. Rolling green hills, covered in green trees of Orange, Fig, Holm Oak, Carobs, Palms and Olives, gently sloping to distant sea views, with the most magnificent sunsets imaginable. We asked Fernando, who owned the land and he said he did! So we sold the original house and built one similar but slightly larger on the new plot. The new house is called 'Casa Travessa Do Pastor' which means the 'House on the Shepherds Crossing' as when we first moved in to the house, the local shepherd would drive his flock up the track and graze his sheep in our garden.

Furnishing both homes soon after the Salazar revolution was a mind broadening experience which is one we are not likely to forget. The wonderful Portuguese attitude to their traditional food and relationship with alcohol has been different and refreshing especially comparing them with the UK. Whilst the food will never be our most favourite in the world, we never have been served poor quality and it has always been wholesome with generous portions.

The enormous changes as a result of entering the EU, at times were so fast it made our head spin trying to keep up. The increase in quality and choice of goods and services has been such good news for the Portuguese who have embraced these changes with welcomed excitement and enthusiasm. The new technologies in communication has improved the lives of all the locals (and us) in ways they could never imagined twenty seven years ago.

Cheap air travel has transformed the tourist industry to the benefit of all who have been involved and given new and exciting jobs to thousands of Algarvian's. The changes to the road systems and the increasing affluence of people, whereby locals have been able to buy motor cars and be much more adventurous with their travel, has been a boon to people and revolutionised their lives.

The weather has continued to be an absolute joy with its warm temperatures, temperate breezes and cool nights. Portugal's entry into the EU has been a life saver to all who have benefited by it, however so many of the changes are causing pain to the administrators, politicians and police who are struggling to understand and comply with the new conditions; but hopefully all of these will be resolved eventually.

Some of the characters we have met over the years have kept us in fits of laughter and disbelief at some of their antics and the local country people continue to be a delight. As an old friend of ours coined a phrase 'Keep your eyes open and its worth a Guinea a minute' It is also refreshing to see that so many of the old traditions, customs and cultures are still respected and still in place, in an ever changing world.

Finally, when we first came to the Algarve in 1984, George Orwell film 'Big Brother is Watching You' and his predictions about the state of the world was wrong. There was no Big Brother watching us in Portugal at that time but his visions were to be partly realised later in the UK, with the advent of public security cameras. Let's hope that the Algarve does not go the same way!

Our favourite Portuguese wine 'Mateus Ros'e.

Having experienced all our situations over the past twenty seven years, both good and bad, would we do the same thing again?

You bet we would!

Well; having now read our book, we hope that you have enjoyed it, and discovered a little bit about the Algarve, which you may not have known before. Also we hope that it has brought a smile to your lips, as it did to ours when we wrote some sections.

If you have liked the book, please tell all your friends to go out and buy copies for themselves and their friends, as all profits will be diverted to the ME fund for impoverished writers.

If you have not liked it, do not let us know, as we would probably end up crying into our wine glass!

THE END